Steve Maricelli, Vice President Demar Engineering and Construction-"An incredible narrative with fascinating insight so real you will believe you are there. A must read."

Chuck Cummings, CPA, CFE-"The author's uncanny ability to observe current events and foresee a plausible explanation of the ancient manuscripts that predict the coming end of the world as we know it, certainly stimulates one's thinking."

L.W. Dyke, Internationally known professional artist-"This is a factually based, well documented wake-up call about the end of this world; it will make you think or just plain frighten you!"

Rick Carr, LtCol. Ret. USAF; Retired Airline Captain who was airborne 9/11/2001-"Powerful. . .Insightful. . .A compelling read!"

Escaping Armageddon

Learn the Secret to Surviving the End of the World

James Bouvier

James Bouvier

Signs of the times

Matt. 16:3

CROSSBOOKS
PUBLISHING

CONTACT: 713 501 6640

bouvierj@sbcgbbal.net

CrossBooks™
A Division of LifeWay
1663 Liberty Drive
Bloomington, IN 47403
www.crossbooks.com
Phone: 1-866-879-0502

First published by CrossBooks 01/25/2011

ISBN: 978-1-6150-7624-6 (sc)
Library of Congress Control Number: 2010939429

Printed in the United States of America
This book is printed on acid-free paper.

This book is dedicated to: my wife Sharon for her love and unwavering support in our forty-three years of marriage and for her overwhelming labor of love in helping me make this book possible; to our son Steven and daughter in law Amy; and to their two children, our precious grandchildren, Riley Alan Bouvier, and Grace Irene Bouvier. Although neither of our grandchildren is able to read this book today (Riley is seven years old and Grace is four years old), they are our future, our legacy and the future lighthouses to a world looking for direction.

James E. Bouvier

Lighthouse in the storm
Painting by J.E. Bouvier

Contents

ACKNOWLEDGEMENTS

Sharon Bouvier-I could never have completed *Escaping Armageddon* without the tireless support, sacrificial hard work and never ending encouragement to proceed with the project by my best friend and wife Sharon. No one will ever know how many times she read, discussed and corrected the endless number of draft manuscripts I manufactured during the four years that I was seriously writing the book since 9/11. She brought out a new dimension of humility in me with each new set of corrections and raised the bar on my ability to take constructive criticism. There were many times when I was at a loss for the right words and a chapter would not have been completed if she had not persisted in telling me to "go back to the computer and figure it out. You are the writer!" Sharon thank you for everything, I really appreciate all you did to make the book possible.

Steve Maricelli-Steve is one of my best friends and has been a constant source of encouragement to me while I was writing the book. He has taken the time to read several of the many drafts of the manuscripts over the years and offered constructive comments on the content and presentation which ultimately made the book stronger and more appealing.

Larry Dyke-Larry is a close friend and provided wise counsel critical to the writing of the book.

Dr. Jim Hastings-Jim took considerable time to provide an essential, very critical review of the manuscript for historical content, readability, appeal and overall apocalyptic accuracy.

Chuck Cummings-The book was strengthened considerably by Chuck's comments following his time consuming review of the manuscript for apocalyptic content and overall subject matter.

Chuck Schneider-Chuck read one of the earlier drafts of the manuscript. Although the book needed a lot of work at that time Chuck was very inspirational and provided comments that actually encouraged me to change the course and perspective of the book.

Alan Elliott-Alan is a good friend, my daughter in law's dad and a computer professional that provided invaluable help with the electronic processing of the manuscript and the development of the website.

Sandra Lengefeld-Sandra exercised her high school English teacher credentials to turn the pages of the draft manuscript red with the necessary corrections for grammar and readability. As a result, the book is more readable and grammatically correct unless I made additional errors incorporating her comments.

Dr. John Morgan- Dr. Morgan will never know the impact on the writing of this book as a result of a few very simple but profound comments he made during our first discussion of the manuscript. Because he took the time to discuss the subject of the book and provide counsel on several important points, the writing turned a critical corner resulting in a more successful book.

Many friends-I appreciate the constant encouragement of so many friends to pursue publishing the book and their relentless interest as to when the book would be completed and available for them to read.

INTRODUCTION

**DANGER-ELECTRICAL SHOCK!
WARNING-BRIDGE OUT!
CAUTION-MAY BE HAZARDOUS
TO YOUR HEALTH!**

*W*arning signs are pleads to heed that we often disregard and fail to respect on a regular basis for one reason or another. In many cases warnings can now be provided well in advance of impending disaster due to the use of available sophisticated technology, giving us additional time to prepare a way of escape–but only if we heed the warning. For example, Harry Truman, a longtime resident on the shores of Spirit Lake in the shadow of Mount St. Helens, was repeatedly warned to leave his home in 1980. Seismological instruments had been indicating to scientists for some time that an eruption of the nearby mountain was imminent. However, Harry stubbornly maintained that the warning was just an empty threat even as the foundation of his home began to tremble. While many residents fled to safety, Harry and others who refused to leave died that day. The rest is history!

Many times danger is either not apparent to us or we don't embrace the possibility of disaster because the reality of adversity impacting us seems unlikely or just downright impossible. I have personally experienced several lethal hurricanes which struck the Texas Gulf Coast. In many instances, people in the strike zone ignored the repeated warnings of weather forecasters and refused to evacuate their homes until the escape routes were impassable due to high water. As residents continued to ignore the threat of dangerous weather closing in from the Gulf of Mexico, blue skies over Texas began to boil with the ominous storm clouds of an approaching deadly hurricane. Ultimately, the hurricane force winds and flooding resulted in the unnecessary loss of life. Why do we reject warnings given to protect us from danger?

Although the warning of approaching cataclysmic global destruction eludes most of the world, ancient manuscripts written thousands of years ago clearly reveal an unprecedented description of the coming apocalypse. *Escaping Armageddon* reveals the true account of the imminent electrifying invasion of earth from beyond our world climaxing with Armageddon and the end of the human race. We are now rushing towards the intersection of current world events and the fulfillment of the last of the ancient prophecies which will initiate the launch of the apocalyptic invasion.

This non-fiction book is a thrilling account of a true narrative based on facts given to us by a supernatural being from another dimension having mysterious powers to accurately foretell the future! Regardless of your background, education, or beliefs, the shocking description of the invasion of our planet will hopefully compel you to discover the secret to escaping Armageddon and surviving the end of the world.

1

SIGNS

---

*N*o one was prepared for the attack on Pearl Harbor at 7:55 AM on a quiet Sunday morning, December 7, 1941. More recently, the nation was shocked when four commercial airliners hijacked by terrorists ripped open the cloudless skies over New York City, Washington D.C., and Pennsylvania with a masterfully orchestrated and devastating blow to America on September 11, 2001. Although each attack caught the United States by complete surprise and thrust Americans into a costly war involving much of the world, there were warning signs of imminent disaster. However, in each case, it was unimaginable that an enemy was capable of successfully attacking America, the most powerful nation in the world. Consequently, some signs were ignored, some were misinterpreted and some just went unnoticed.

On two unforgettable days separated by almost sixty years of colorful history, Americans were reminded that life is fragile and that disaster can come to the unsuspecting from an unexpected, unbelievable, and totally unprecedented attack. A surprise attack will always reap the most deadly results. The failure to recognize and heed the warning signs fosters a false sense of security and may cause procrastination for preparation until it's too late. As the world rushes through the twenty-first century at the speed of life, ominous, dark storm clouds are gathering from the four corners of the planet. Warning signs of an imminent catastrophic event of unparalleled global proportions threaten the destiny of mankind and the end of the world, but does anyone see them?

Natural disasters are delivering devastation to mankind at an alarming and seemingly increasing rate each year. In recent months and years, thousands of people throughout the world have suffered and died from the effects of deadly hurricanes, massive earthquakes, enormous tsunamis, unbelievably lethal volcanic eruptions, and new strains of pandemic flu. It's as if the earth is exercising her revenge for the abuse mankind has caused her over the centuries. Are these deadly attacks of nature a sign of things to come?

In 2007, world financial markets, boasting of prosperity and unparalleled wealth, promptly followed the United States in a sudden, massive meltdown resulting in a global recession. Trillions of dollars literally evaporated overnight, financially devastating businesses and the lives and dreams of families around the world. Millions of Americans lost their jobs, their homes, and their life savings as unemployment in the nation soared above ten percent. They lost confidence in their political leaders in Washington and the system of checks and balances designed to protect markets from such a disaster. The outcry of Americans voicing their anger with the legislative process of Congress and the White House surged to a critical level, threatening to divide the nation. Many businesses and even icons of the American automobile industry filed for bankruptcy, while some nations, like Greece, looked to the European Union to save them from economic failure. The unparalleled spending by the United States government prompted several countries to demand a global currency to replace the depreciating dollar. While financial markets recovered somewhat in 2010, people throughout the world continued to struggle. Is this disastrous world event a warning of a coming global catastrophe that could result in the total collapse of world markets?

The world is literally a powder keg requiring only a spark of aggression from a rogue nation for ignition. For years, the United States has been recognized as the most powerful nation on earth, commanding a position of respect and authority throughout the world. Historically, we have had a military second to none and a commander-in-chief who would not hesitate to defend the democracy of our nation and the brave men and women who protect the freedom we cherish. However, the White House administration of 2009 has chosen to join nations who are willing to lay their "swords on the table" in the name of peace and soft political diplomacy, while other countries aggressively pursue the development of weapons of mass destruction.

Iran is on a razor-sharp edge of having weapons-grade nuclear material suitable for the construction of a bomb. The President of Iran vowed to wipe Israel "off the map" and will soon have the weapons to execute that threat. North Korea recently conducted tests of nuclear bombs and successfully test-fired rockets capable of deploying nuclear warheads to the shores of America. The day is also rapidly approaching when the world will grow tired of the Middle East holding the global economy hostage with the supply of oil—the black gold of the twenty-first century which powers the engines of progress. Is the changing political and military climate of the planet warning us that the balance of power between nations is shifting to a dangerous position, making the feared possibility of nuclear war an actual reality? The world is a ticking time bomb.

We're in the midst of a world in turmoil which seems to be hopelessly spinning out of control and threatening to self-destruct. There are even grassroots organizations encouraging the stockpiling of food, water, and other supplies in anticipation of severe shortages. Americans in every walk of life are searching for the secret to protect the quality and security of their future from the threat of the unknown. People strain to see a light of hope somewhere in the darkness of uncertainty. If only we had a sneak preview of the future, we could begin to chart a new course for our lives today in order to avoid the pitfalls of danger, to take advantage of opportunities, and to ensure a happier, safer tomorrow.

Unfortunately, mankind has historically been unsuccessful in its attempts to lift the veil of the present and gaze into the future with any accuracy. However, there is one true, factual account of the destiny of planet earth and the future of the human race clearly documented in ancient manuscripts written thousands of years ago. Included in these manuscripts is mysterious insider information that provides a detailed description of the most bizarre event in the history of mankind, and we are warned that it is coming soon. This relevant and ominous but obscure warning of disaster is known and understood by relatively few people in the world today and will be a shocking surprise. Shrouded in mysterious symbols and code words, this chronicle of the future reveals an unimaginable, deadly invasion of the earth from beyond this planet. We have been given little knowledge of the exact time this attack will occur, although we have a detailed account of how it will happen, how long it will last, and the magnitude of the resulting death toll. We have also been given mysterious signs and coded messages in the manuscripts that provide clues to the identity of the generation targeted for this attack. I believe we may be that generation—the "terminal generation."

2

THE DAY WE CAN
NEVER FORGET

"*G*ood evening again, this is your captain from the flight deck. We are approximately forty miles east of Houston, Texas, and have started our final approach into Houston Intercontinental Airport. The weather in Houston is a sweltering ninety degrees with light winds out of the southwest at six miles an hour with scattered clouds. On behalf of the entire flight crew, we thank you for flying with us today and hope you have a pleasant stay in Houston or the place of your final destination." Whether you're a seasoned frequent flyer or have just completed your first trip on a commercial airliner, you have likely heard this kind of announcement from the cockpit sometime near the end of your flight. Of course, the comment was only a cordial expression from the crew for you to enjoy your stay in the place of your scheduled destination. However, the phrase *final destination* can have a certain ring of a foreboding, irrevocable finality to it.

It's a fact that everyone intends to reach their planned destinations each day and rarely considers the possibility of not arriving at all. Although many people live as though they will live forever, life is uncertain, and there is no guarantee of another breath, much less another day of life. Sadly, that ring of finality became reality on September 11, 2001, in one day of unmitigated terror. On that unforgettable day, almost three thousand innocent people were unknowingly thrust into the cross-hairs of terrorist weapons and were launched to what became their real and final destination. The bureaucratic governmental agencies responsible for the safety of American citizens failed to properly "connect the dots" of numerous obscure signs and warnings that would have provided evidence of a planned attack on the United States. The surprise 9/11 tragedy was a regrettable lesson in the consequences of failing to recognize and adequately analyze the significance of signs and warnings, so that preparation can be made to avoid, or at least minimize, impending disaster.

The attack on the World Trade Center, September 11, 2001[1]
New York City, New York

8

THE DAY WE CAN NEVER FORGET

ANOTHER DAY AT THE OFFICE

Shortly before 9:00 AM on September 11, 2001, people were sitting at their desks in the two World Trade Center buildings in New York City having their first cup of coffee and bagel. It was supposed to be just another day at the office. Scores of others were working their way up from the subway system located in the cavernous bowels of the building complex far below the street level. That was a familiar routine for me when I traveled from Houston, Texas, to New York City on business and worked in an office in the South Tower of the World Trade Center for several days at a time.

I began each day by taking the subway to the World Trade Center complex. On arrival at the station, I made my way up the escalators from the subterranean subway platform to the street level of the twin tower complex. Occasionally, I paused as I stepped off the escalator at the top and looked down to the subway station several stories below. During the morning rush hours, the multiple parallel banks of escalators were packed with people standing shoulder-to-shoulder as they slowly rose from the depths below on the moving stairway. I was intrigued by the endless flow of people. It was as though there was some kind of bizarre factory in the core of the earth, tirelessly manufacturing neatly dressed business people and delivering them in assembly-line fashion to the street.

The people stood motionless on the ride up the escalators. Some of them appeared to be asleep. They filed off at the top and joined others to form what looked like a massive human river flowing slowly but deliberately out to the lobby of the complex and into the street. Then as if every move was being orchestrated by some higher power, the river of bodies split into dozens of small streams and tributaries that twisted and turned around every corner. The people disappeared into nearby

9

buildings or joined those on the crowded sidewalks bound for other destinations. In the evening this routine was reversed. The army of tired workers and weary tourists filed slowly onto the moving staircase and disappeared into the shadows of the vast depths below.

Once I reached the street level, I was met with all the sights, smells and sounds of New York City in the early morning hours. There were the never-ending sirens, the drone of what seemed like a million people talking at once, the incessant honking of horns, and the smell of fresh bagels and hot coffee. The streets seemed to be painted yellow with the flood of the infamous New York City taxis, and everyone was in a hurry. I would often stop to gaze at the unique Sphere standing in the plaza of the World Trade Center. This unusual looking globe was originally conceived as a symbol of world peace. The Sphere, visibly wounded by the merciless attack, now stands bravely on guard in Battery Park in the shadow of the site of the twin towers, to memorialize all those who lost their lives to the terrorists on that infamous day.

The Sphere in Battery Park[2]
New York City, New York

I made my way into one of the crowded elevators of the lobby to reach the floor where I was working. I also enjoyed an occasional lunch in the Windows on the World Restaurant, which was a popular tourist attraction located on the 106th and 107th floors of the North Tower. Floor to ceiling windows around the entire periphery of the area gave an amazing panoramic view of the New York City skyline, New York harbor and the Statue of Liberty. It was fascinating to look out the windows and see aircraft flying below me making their final approach to one of the nearby airports.

In September 2001, I was working on a project in the financial district near the World Trade Center. I returned to Houston the Friday before the attack and was scheduled to fly back to New York City Tuesday morning, September 11, 2001. However, due to a change in my work schedule I didn't make the trip and I escaped harm's way. I was made aware of what happened as I joined a crowd of co-workers glued to a television and witnessing the attack firsthand.

It was a beautiful day in the Northeast on September 11, 2001. Skies were absolutely blue and crystal clear. People in the offices of the twin towers were preparing for the day's activities just like they had done every other day. Some people may have been thinking about what they would do when they returned home that evening. Some may not have taken the time to say "goodbye" or "I love you" to that special person before they left. How often have we all done something similar? How many times have we left home without doing the important things believing we will take care of them when we return?

> *Don't put off those all important things that mean so much to others just to meet the demands of never ending business schedules or to satisfy people whose only interest in you is what you can do for them today. It sounds trite but it only takes a few minutes to do what you know you should do. When those few minutes pass, they're gone. Who knows whether life will offer a few minutes to us again at a later date? You just can't count on it. Your motto should be "Do it now!" Remember, you will never pass exactly this same way ever again!*

On that fateful September 11 morning at approximately 8:45 AM, American Airlines Flight 11, which had just left Boston's Logan Airport bound for Los Angeles, departed from its intended flight path and proceeded directly on a collision course with the 110-story North Tower of the World Trade Center. The aircraft with its tanks loaded with jet fuel literally disappeared into the building creating a holocaust out of a world-renowned cornerstone for the financial district of the United States. The entire world focused on the live television pictures of smoke and destruction generated by the first attack on the World Trade Center. Initially, this attack was believed to be an accident, but that idea was soon dismissed.

Although the first crash was a complete surprise and escaped the eyes of many Americans, the second one did not. In fact, most of the world was riveted to live television coverage of the twin towers by that time. At approximately 9:00 AM United Airlines Flight 175, which left Logan

Airport bound for Los Angeles, crashed into the South Tower of the World Trade Center. The aircraft was skillfully guided into the building, wings tilted steeply so as to maximize penetration of the building and generate the full force of the exploding jet fuel carried by the aircraft. It seemed at first that the most dramatic scene in New York City would be the smoke and flames boiling from the two World Trade Center towers. The focus of dramatic media coverage was on the men and women fighting the fire and rescuing those trapped in the burning buildings. Many heroes were made that day and many died saving others. Then totally and unexpectedly at approximately 9:50 AM as the world watched on live television in horror, the South Tower of the World Trade Center began to collapse, one floor falling on top of another like a house of cards. A few minutes later the second tower began to collapse. In a matter of minutes the World Trade Center tower complex, an icon standing proudly for New York City and the United States was gone.

At approximately 9:45 AM several hundred miles to the south of New York City, American Airlines Flight 77, which left Dulles International Airport in Washington D.C. bound for Los Angeles, made a turn back toward the city and crashed into the west side of the Pentagon where more innocent lives were taken without warning. A few minutes later United Airlines Flight 93, which left Newark Liberty Airport bound for San Francisco, crashed in a vacant field in rural Pennsylvania. This aircraft, also under the control of hijackers, crashed as a result of the heroic crew and many brave passengers successfully foiling the attempts of the terrorists to fly the plane into another of their intended targets. A brave flight crew and an aircraft filled with American heroes posing as passengers gave their lives so that another terrorist attack on an unsuspecting, innocent target could be averted. The terrorists planned to sacrifice their lives and destroy Americans. They never counted on heroic Americans willing to sacrifice their lives to prevent the terrorists from reaching their target.

The nation was united that day for a cause that could not have been imagined hours earlier. People cried for the loss of those they didn't know and vowed angrily to retaliate against the perpetrators at all cost. The giant World Trade Center buildings, standing tall and proud overlooking the New York harbor minutes before were reduced to a massive pile of disintegrated concrete and twisted steel. The Pentagon that had been a beehive of activity minutes earlier now had a gaping black smoking hole in the side of it. A scorched field in western Pennsylvania littered with debris from the crash of the fourth hijacked airliner was all that remained to testify to the heroics of the crew and passengers on United Airlines Flight 93.

Twice in American history a surprise attack, both thought to be impossible if not highly unlikely, has been necessary to awaken this giant of a nation slumbering under the comfortable covers of prosperity and complacency. Because of this shocking attack America will never be the same; Americans will never be the same. We should never be the same. September 11, 2001 was the day we can never forget. It will be a constant reminder to watch for warning signs of imminent danger and always expect the unexpected and be prepared for the impossible.

A WAKE-UP CALL

The 9/11 assault on America was a resounding wake-up call; America was caught off guard by a magnificently orchestrated surprise attack. Special investigative groups sifted tirelessly through the mountain of historical intelligence memos, tapes and files, searching for clues that could reveal how the 9/11 plot was so masterfully designed and flawlessly executed. They looked for cracks in the infrastructure of our global intelligence systems that did not recognize this breach of national security. More importantly, why was there a failure to connect-the-dots of the terrorists' preparation for the attack that was executed right here in the United States? Would the outcome have been any different if the signs and warnings had been more obvious, required less analysis and provided the necessary information in time to stop the attack or, at least, make a way of escape? Of course! The nation may not have totally avoided tragedy, but people would certainly have been better prepared.

Several years have now passed since 9/11. Our nation struggles to strengthen the security of our airports, borders, ports of entry and other potentially vulnerable areas to minimize the possibility of another terrorist attack. Solid countermeasures are promptly implemented by the government as soon as new terrorist techniques for destruction are utilized in a deadly act. However, it seems that inadequate resources are expended to seek out and identify the warning signs and proactively develop safeguards for new, more innovative methods of terrorism before they're used to kill innocent victims. As recently as December 25, 2009, a terrorist known as the "the underpants bomber" attempted to blow up Northwest Airlines Flight 253 from Amsterdam to Detroit. The attack was foiled only by a faulty igniter for the explosives and brave passengers on the aircraft. A second attack occurred in May 2010 in Times Square, New York City and was also thwarted by a faulty igniter for the explosives. It's as if the terrorists are saying, "We're alive and well, catch us if you can!" Does anyone see the warning signs? Doing a great job of explaining an attack after the fact will never protect victims and save lives.

In an attempt to break the backs and spirits of Americans, the terrorists initially united us with an unquenchable thirst to defend the freedom and shores of our country. However, as the stark reality of 9/11 faded over the years, the nation's political leaders deserted the commitment made by the President of the United States to boldly support the war on terror and debated the value of our involvement in the Middle-East. The once unified cry of the politicians backed by the American voters to defend this great nation against any enemy at all cost was reduced to a muffled voice and tacit approval of the war on terror. During 2008, the year of the presidential election in the United States, news reporting of the progress of the war in the Middle East was reduced to little more than background noise as terrorists continued to ravage the world.

It seems many of our nation's leaders have forgotten their primary obligation to the citizens of the United States of America is to defend our freedom and protect us from the threat of our enemies, regardless of the cost. The desire of many of our elected officials in Washington is to balance our freedom on the basis of peaceful diplomacy with our enemies who bear false promises rather than maintaining the strength and military presence that made our nation great.

In 2009, less than a month after the newly elected President of the United States took office, the Executive Office discussed a reduction in the budget for the military while we struggled to admit we were at war with terrorists. In the next few months, cordial speeches and gifts were exchanged between our President and dictators of the world in the name of a new American foreign policy framed with unparalleled "soft diplomacy." Apologies were made for the past actions of America to some of the very countries that our brave soldiers died fighting to protect. We embarrassed our allies in Poland and the Czech Republic by sacrificing the installation of a missile defense system planned in their countries that would protect them as well as preserve our national security in exchange for empty promises from Russia.

This relatively unknown, charismatic diplomat emerged from the shadows of politics, boldly marched up the steps to the White House of our great nation and promised to fundamentally change America. Since the day he took office, he kept that promise, clearly charting a new course for the future of the United States. However, if the politicians allow our nation to become vulnerable to future attacks by terrorists and other enemies, it will be an abomination to our American heroes, including my father, who gave their lives for the freedom of all Americans. Indeed, social issues and a decent standard of living are important, even critical, to each of us. But how important are they, if we lose our freedom to work, to live and to worship? Have we learned anything?

Ironically, it only takes another act of terror against the United States for the nation and its leaders to bend their knees once again and cry out for help. On November 10, 2009, the nation paused to remember thirteen fallen U.S. Army soldiers who made the ultimate sacrifice for their country. However, these military heroes were not killed on the battlefields in Afghanistan or Iraq; this surprise attack occurred within the very borders of the "secure" United States Army Base at Fort Hood in Killeen, Texas on November 5, 2009. Their lives were taken suddenly by a rogue shooter who, in fact, was an officer in the U.S. Army. Many believe he had ties to radical extremists and that America is becoming a breeding ground for homegrown terrorists. We may be living and working shoulder-to-shoulder with the "enemy" at home. It's unfortunate that it takes tragedy to occasionally stir our nation from the slumber of complacency, only to have it soon turn over and go comfortably back to sleep.

Our symbol of liberty, New York City, New York
Photograph by J.E. Bouvier

We have been given a wake-up call by these attacks on our great nation, and we need to recognize the signs and heed the warnings in order to be better prepared next time. More importantly, the ancient manuscripts of the insider information have given us a clear, unmistakable warning compelling the world to prepare now for the ultimate global surprise attack that is on a collision course with earth. I doubt there is one person who would have chosen to be in the towers, the Pentagon or a passenger on one of the ill-fated aircraft that fateful September day if given advance information of an imminent attack.

3

WE HAVE BEEN WARNED

*R*egardless of the preemptive signs and warnings, the surprise 9/11 attack on America was regretfully successful and tragically ended the lives of thousands of innocent people. However, while the nation was still reeling from the devastation of 9/11, another tragedy shocked Americans and rocked the world. The lives of seven brave astronauts were taken suddenly as the space shuttle Columbia rocketed toward a heroes' welcome following a successful mission in space. This time there was neither a warning of impending danger nor any tell-tale signs that could have forecast this disaster. The astronauts would have welcomed a warning or signs of approaching danger, allowing them time to execute an escape. Unfortunately, the crew of the Columbia had neither!

MINUTES FROM ARRIVAL

On the morning of February 1, 2003, my wife and I were driving north on Interstate Highway 45 from

Houston, Texas toward Dallas. We noticed what looked like a commercial aircraft flying high in the clear blue sky, glistening in the sunlight heading toward the eastern horizon. It was a common sight to see commercial aircraft crisscrossing the Texas skies at high altitude. Each airplane customarily painted a thin, straight white condensation line on a canvas of blue sky, characteristic of aircraft flying in the extreme cold air of high altitude. In fact, it was the condensation trail from this aircraft in a sky uninhabited by any other airliners at the time that caught our attention. The white trail from this craft was unusually thick, fluffy and somewhat erratic, not at all normal-looking for any aircraft.

Launch of Columbia[1]
January 16, 2003

As the aircraft streaked across the sky, we suddenly realized this was not a conventional airplane, and it was definitely in distress. The Columbia was scheduled to land at Cape Canaveral in Florida in a few minutes, which put the spacecraft directly overhead on a flight path across Central Texas and Louisiana. We suddenly but sadly realized we were eyewitnesses to the flight of the troubled space shuttle Columbia. The crew must have been making a feverish effort to safely reach the scheduled landing area which was only a few minutes away at the speed the craft was traveling. We later heard on the radio that NASA had lost all contact with the shuttle which had successfully re-entered the earth's atmosphere earlier.

It seemed as though the flight path of Columbia, which looked unusually erratic, was taking place in slow motion. Seconds seemed like minutes. As Columbia passed the mid-point of our horizon, parts of the spacecraft seemed to rip off the main body accompanied by bright flashes of eerie green light, looking like a supernatural sparkler in the early morning light. Columbia suddenly broke into several large pieces with the fragments continuing to rocket across the horizon until they were out of sight. We learned later that debris from the ill-fated spacecraft was scattered over hundreds of square miles of northeast Texas and Louisiana.

This scene was etched in our minds forever as we later learned that seven brave astronauts had been launched to their final destination in eternity when something went tragically wrong on that flight. The magnificent marvel of man's technology lost a valiant battle to deliver the crew safely to their families and friends waiting expectantly in Florida. The anticipation of celebration of another successful mission in space turned to disbelief, panic, shock and then grief. How could this tragedy happen with so many people working so diligently to ensure the safety of the crew?

Post-launch photographic analysis indicated insulating foam separated from the external fuel tank and struck one wing of Columbia, causing the loss of tiles which protect the shuttle from searing heat during re-entry. Unfortunately, the loss of tiles was not noticed "real time." Finally, the failure of several on board sensors in the damaged wing of Columbia during re-entry was assumed to be an instrumentation problem rather than a sign of impending disaster. By this time the shuttle was several minutes from the intended landing site, all communication between the ground and Columbia was lost and the sequence for destruction of Columbia had been activated. The rest is history!

The world that had grown complacent with so many successful space shuttle flights now stood silent. President George W. Bush stood before the American people once again with the heart-breaking memory of 9/11 still fresh in everyone's minds. He gave the eulogy for those who had given their lives for the future of science. At the national memorial service held at the Johnson Space Center February 4, 2003, President Bush said, "The men and women of the *Columbia* had journeyed more than six million miles and were minutes away from arrival and reunion. The loss was sudden and terrible, and for their families, the grief is heavy. Our nation shares in your sorrow and in your pride."[2] I'm sure none of the seven astronauts had any idea when they woke that morning that they would see their last sunrise.

The occurrence of a catastrophic disaster without warning is not unusual. In the year 2000, my wife and I were visiting Paris, France. We awoke one morning to hear the news that a Concorde jet crashed just outside Paris a few miles from the Charles de Gaulle Airport. Before that day, the sleek futuristic-looking Concorde jet had a thirty-year untarnished reputation for flying safety. However, on that fateful morning, Concorde Flight AF4590 burst into flames without warning during takeoff and crashed a few minutes later in a ball of fire killing everyone on board, as well as several unsuspecting residents on the ground. No one on that aircraft had any warning that their lives would end suddenly in a barren field outside Paris, France, just three minutes after taking off on the world's safest, fastest commercial jet airliner.

We can do little to prepare for disaster when there is no warning, as in the sudden destruction of the space shuttle Columbia and the fiery crash of the Concorde. Therefore, warning signs of impending danger should be recognized as gifts and taken seriously. We must learn to trust warnings and heed them, regardless of whether we see or even believe the possibility of danger. Warning signs may simply help us avoid an accident in a dangerous intersection, prevent us from crossing the path of a speeding locomotive in a death race we cannot win, or avoid the most terrifying global assault on mankind in the history of the world. When our safety and security are at stake, warnings cannot be ignored. The ancient manuscripts of the insider information are screaming an unmistakably clear warning that the imminent invasion of planet earth from beyond our world will bring unparalleled devastation to mankind. The signs are everywhere; we have been warned, but will we heed the warning?

HISTORY REPEATS ITSELF

We still have time to prepare a way of escape and survive the end of the world. Unfortunately, history tends to repeat itself. There will be many people who hear and understand the warning but ignore it because a global invasion of earth sounds both unimaginable and impossible. After all, there is no civilization on earth or known life-form with the capability to stage such an attack on earth. Does that mean it can't happen? There are many practical examples of events that have happened in our own lifetime that seemed unlikely or even impossible just a few years ago. Who would have believed the following events could take place?

1. Scientists would learn the secret of splitting the atom and use it for peaceful purposes as well as the development of nuclear weapons that abruptly ended WW II in 1945.

2. The Berlin Wall constructed in1961would fall in 1989.

3. Man would set foot on the moon and return safely to earth in 1969.

4. The powerful U.S.S.R. would be broken up in 1991.

5. Terrorists would attack America using four commercial airliners as weapons of mass destruction September 11, 2001.

Look closely at the following relevant case in recent history where the clear warning of a surprise catastrophic attack was given in advance of certain destruction but ignored. The consequences of ignoring the warning were difficult, if not impossible, to believe but proved to be very real and deadly. Several days before the United States dropped the first atomic bomb on Hiroshima in August 1945, an ultimatum called the Potsdam Declaration was delivered to the Japanese minister, Shigenori Togo. President Truman said, "We call upon the government of Japan to proclaim now that unconditional surrender of all Japanese armed forces, and to provide proper and adequate assurances of their good faith in such action. The alternative for Japan is prompt and utter destruction... That afternoon the B-29s came to Hiroshima as they came to so many other Japanese cities. But they did not bring bombs. They brought leaflets, tens of thousands of them, each one carrying the Japanese text of the Potsdam Declaration."[3] The leaflets from the high flying silver B29 aircraft warned the Japanese people of Hiroshima and Nagasaki, the two target cities, of the impending destruction of life and property if Japan rejected the ultimatum from the United States for an unconditional surrender. However, the leaflets did not explain how the destruction would come or precisely when it would come. Even though there was a clear warning of impending disaster, the actual time and method of devastation was unknown to the Japanese and would be a surprise. Of course, the warning was ignored, Japan refused the unconditional surrender and "... a quarter of a million people died as a result of the two atomic bombs dropped..."[4] The rest is history!

Hopefully, the description of the massive global assault on earth documented in the ancient manuscripts will convince you this warning cannot be ignored. This surprise attack cannot be stopped or altered and it will happen precisely as it's predicted. Millions, perhaps billions of people, will die and the earth will be decimated but we know in advance it's going to happen.

You may ask why hasn't there been anything about this predicted mysterious invasion of the earth in the daily newspapers. Why hasn't it been discussed on the nightly television news or debated on the popular talk shows? In this day and age when the popular topics are the financial crisis, politics, corporate greed, scandal, stardom, disasters, war and foreign affairs, this subject just hasn't made it to the news. It will someday! Where did the ominous warning come from and who gave it to us? We have to go back about two thousand years in time to discover the truth about the future.

4

BACK 2000 YEARS
TO THE FUTURE

---

*W*all Street in lower Manhattan, New York City, New York is a household word throughout America and many parts of the world, synonymous with the stock market and the workplace for those investing in stocks, bonds and other securities. The secret to making money in the stock market is simply to buy low and sell high. However, some people take advantage of what's called insider information known only to those on the "inside" of a company. This privileged information usually describes future events which will cause the price of a stock to increase or decrease dramatically. If an investor can obtain this advance information about a financial security, he is likely to capitalize on the future. Of course, the use of valuable insider information by anyone for personal gain is illegal since it is not available for use by the general public.

However, about two thousand years ago, the world was given an incredible journal containing an ominous warning about future events. This fascinating chronicle reveals the shocking details of the most horrifying seven years in the history of mankind-the invasion of planet earth culminating in the battle of Armageddon and the end of the world. This little-known insider information was actually sent by a mysterious being from another dimension to encourage everyone living in the generation targeted by the invasion to freely capitalize on the future by preparing the way of escape. Therefore, regardless of your beliefs or skepticism, the graphic description of the imminent annihilation of the human race and the destruction of our planet merits an intensely compelling reason to understand the warning and discover the key to the secret to surviving the end of the world.

THE END OF THE WORLD

People are fascinated with movies and literary works that dramatize fictional accounts of the destruction of the world by natural disasters, rogue asteroids and even alien life-forms from deep space. The entertainment world is mesmerized with each new book and movie that capitalizes on the exciting heart-stopping themes of Armageddon and the Apocalypse. As a result, disciples of doomsday predictions are quick to embrace prophecies featuring signs that signal the end of the world. Some people characterized the traumatic events of September 11, 2001, as one step in a sequence that will ultimately lead to Armageddon and the demise of planet earth. Others believe the massive meltdown of global financial markets in 2008 was a definite sign of the beginning of the end. The blockbuster movie *2012* launched in 2009 captivated the imagination of millions of people and stimulated their interest in the latest prophecy for the end of the world. The movie, which is based on an ancient Mayan calendar, portrays the destruction of the world caused by a catastrophic chain of unprecedented natural disasters predicted to begin on December 21, 2012.

What is the truth about Armageddon and the end of the world? Will the earth actually be destroyed someday and, if so, by what or whom? Is there an advanced alien life-form from another galaxy in deep space preparing to invade our world? Does life come to an end due to natural disasters as predicted by the Mayans? Is there any way of escape? The insider information answers all these questions and more in the only true account of the future and destiny of mankind.

INSIDER INFORMATION

Who hasn't wanted to get a glimpse of the future so changes could be made in the paths and timing of one's life to avoid a life-threatening experience like a car accident or to take advantage of a once-in-a-lifetime opportunity, like winning the lottery? Travel to the future is an exciting fantasy of mankind fictionalized in countless books and movies to stimulate the imagination of would-be time travelers. Even Jules Verne dreamed of a machine that could travel through time, allow him to experience the future and then return to the present to make life-changing decisions. Of course, it was only a dream. No one can actually see the future, at least no one in this world! Therefore, the breathtaking "advance copy" of how the world will end fulfills a life-long dream of mankind to experience an event in the future and alter the course of life before the future becomes the present. The good news is the modern day translation of the valuable ancient manuscripts of the future is not buried in rare dusty books or obscure archaic scrolls with faded images and frail pages. This priceless journal of the future from the past is not protected by a glass case in a museum, nor is it guarded by high-tech security systems in a library of invaluable artifacts. In fact, the elusive chronicle is hidden inconspicuously in an inexpensive literary publication that can be found in hundreds of languages in bookstores and libraries in most parts of the free world.

This compilation of ancient manuscripts is a one-of-a-kind volume of history, mystery and secrets to successful living. It accurately documents civilizations of the past, precisely predicts the destiny of a generation of future civilizations, provides proven life changing principles for successful living and reveals the secrets of the mystifying, spiritual world beyond the grave. The foundation and contents of this book are authenticated by centuries of ongoing discoveries and documented historical facts resulting from the tireless work of organizations in science and archeology relentlessly searching for the truth. This timeless literary work contains a unique dimension of knowledge of the past, present and the future that doesn't exist anywhere else in any form, and the message has never been more critically relevant to a generation of people than today. While many of the world's scholars have sought to challenge the truth and accuracy of this unique volume of ancient literature, they have often bowed to the results of historical evidence and become its strongest supporters.

The truth about the fate of the world and the only hope for the ultimate survival of mankind is firmly anchored in one mysterious part of this volume of manuscripts that is often overlooked and disregarded by the layman and even ignored by serious students of ancient literature. However, it's in this apocalyptic text that the amazing insider information is accurately recorded. Although the book may not be familiar to many people, the subject matter continues to tantalize the curiosity of those interested in the truth about Armageddon, the fate of mankind and the end of the world.

Although incredibly shocking and unimaginable, the description of events revealed in this ancient set of records faithfully paints an accurate picture of the future of planet earth and the demise of the human race on a canvas of stark reality. Other ancient manuscripts offer those concerned about their destiny the opportunity to alter the future by revealing the secret to surviving the end of the world. For those who may have difficulty accepting the truth of the ominous warning and the necessity to prepare the way of escape, consider the percentage of all the knowledge in all the books in all the libraries in the world. New information is being generated every minute about our world, new discoveries are being made daily and the number of new books published with a wealth of knowledge is increasing at a phenomenal rate. This doesn't even include the massive amount of information on the internet that's increasing at the speed of new websites and twitter accounts.

If we could stop the explosion of new information, would you possess at least a fraction of one percent of all the knowledge currently existing in the world? Give yourself the benefit of the doubt and assume you know a full one percent. Is it possible that in the ninety-nine percent of the knowledge you lack, the manuscripts of the insider information may hold the truth of the destiny of mankind? Can you set aside skepticism, education and even religious beliefs to consider this warning if it will save your life and the lives of your family? If the Japanese had believed that bizarre but ominous, impossible sounding warning of destruction delivered by America's high flying silver B-29's in 1945 and evacuated the target cities, thousands of lives would have been saved.

THE "INSIDER"

Since the alleged recovery of extra-terrestrial debris from the crash of an alien space-craft near Roswell, New Mexico in 1947, mankind's fascination with the possibility of intelligent life beyond our planet has intensified beyond belief. Scientists and amateurs alike have been captivated by investigations of thousands of sightings of unidentified flying objects (UFO's) alleged to be manned by extra-terrestrial beings. They are spellbound by numerous theories that alien life-forms have visited earth, leaving signs and messages for the world to ponder. The discovery of strange symbols and monuments around the world that are totally foreign to the geography, time period, culture or technology of the day continues to fuel the interest of those searching for hard evidence that extraterrestrial beings have been here. For example, there are hundreds of stone statues weighing more than a hundred tons each and towering more than thirty feet on the remote Easter Island in the southern Pacific Ocean. The origin of these statues which were discovered in 1722 and the civilization that created them continue to be one of the world's unexplained mysteries which many people attribute to an alien visitation.

On a recent visit to England, my wife and I were absolutely mesmerized as we stood on the site of the mysterious geometric placement of massive towering stones called Stonehenge, believed to have been constructed more than 5,000 years ago in Wiltshire County, England. However, scientific and archeological societies are no closer today in completely understanding who constructed this mysterious monument or why it was built than when they started studying it. Some people speculate visitors from outer space may have been responsible for constructing this unexplained wonder of the world.

Stonehenge, Wiltshire England
Photograph by J.E. Bouvier

Then there are the mysterious signs and symbols discovered in the Nazca Desert in Peru which are believed to be more than 1,000 years old. However, the identity of these mammoth signs and symbols that sprawl over acres of ground are only discernable from a balloon, airplane or, some say, an alien spaceship. Why and how did someone create such figures which could only be seen from the sky when there were no vehicles for flight in existence at the time, or were there? However, the alleged alien benefactors of these and many other mysterious signs, symbols and monuments discovered around the world left no evidence of their identity or their homeland. In fact, the timeless mysteries discovered on earth and attributed to unidentified extraterrestrial beings fail to produce any kind of obvious purpose or message for mankind past, present or future. Therefore, the benefactors of the strange shrines from out of this world remain an unsolved mystery.

There is no question about the source of the insider information. There is no mystery that it was provided for the unmistakable specific purpose to clearly warn and ultimately rescue those living in the generation targeted for destruction by the invasion of the planet. However, who was the strange messenger that delivered the incredible knowledge of the future and how did he know it was going to happen? Every civilization and culture has embraced the belief that there is a spiritual force or a higher power that oversees the universe and sits at the controls of our world allowing nature and its laws to take its course. It is believed that this supernatural being monitors the activities of mankind and often intervenes in the lives of individuals. Of course, there has always been speculation and debate as to whom or what this higher power is.

The ancient manuscripts clearly document and identify the source of the mysterious information to be an all-powerful, all-knowing supernatural spiritual being from another dimension whose existence defies all logic, understanding and scientific explanation. It's amazing that this supreme being who has knowledge of the clandestine plot to destroy the world is willing to share that knowledge with the generation targeted for attack. The chronicle of the future included in the collection of ancient manuscripts specifically identifies a man named John as the one to whom the journal of the future was given while he was exiled on the remote island of Patmos. It remains unexplained to this day how the mysterious being was able to communicate detailed visions of the future destruction of earth across two thousand years of space and time to a simple man in the first century A.D.

History, science and archeology have authenticated the fulfillment of other predictions of events recorded in these ancient manuscripts with each occurrence happening exactly as described. Therefore, there is every reason to believe the end of the world will also occur precisely as predicted. The exact time the invasion will begin was not disclosed, but signs, clues and descriptions of events that will precede the attack on earth and clearly point to the time for the beginning of the end were provided.

Coded clues that unlock the secrets to many of the mysteries of the destiny of mankind were revealed to other men by strange visitors to earth hundreds of years before the life-saving information was given to John. Each of these apocalyptic messages were skillfully designed to ultimately fit together perfectly like the pieces of an intricate puzzle. However, no single recipient of clues understood how his piece of the puzzle contributed to the picture that would not completely materialize until thousands of years later. It is totally unimaginable how the mind of this supernatural being could possibly orchestrate such a puzzling presentation of coded messages and clues to generations of people over thousands of years that would one day paint a perfect picture of the future. Therefore, the entire mystery of the invasion of earth, Armageddon and the end of the world will become clear only to the generation targeted for destruction. At that time, all the signs will have been fulfilled, the clues will have been discovered and the prophecies of world events that are precursors to the invasion will have all taken place. I believe we may be the generation seeing the last pieces of the puzzle and the finished picture taking shape; the "terminal generation."

Turn the clock back about two thousand years and meet John, the man who was singled out to receive the insider information. Later, we will travel to the future with John as our narrator and witness the graphic, chilling details of the invasion as well as the horror of the battle of Armageddon and the end of human history.

ALCATRAZ OF THE FIRST CENTURY

John was a simple man in the twilight years of his life living in the ancient bustling city of Ephesus in the first century A.D. He was a champion of religious reform from Israel who had a passion for people. However, his work in Ephesus, a city noted for education, great libraries, and cultural infrastructure located in what is now modern Turkey, was in direct conflict with the mandated worship of the emperor in Rome. Rather than make a martyr of him, the Roman government exiled John to a small, isolated island in the Aegean Sea called Patmos, usually reserved for political prisoners. Patmos could be called the Alcatraz of the first century for without a boat there was no way a person could possibly escape from the island and survive the perils of the sea. With only meager living conditions the loneliness of Patmos was cruel punishment for the prisoners since the island offered nothing to do and nowhere to go.

The remains of the great library in ancient Ephesus
Photograph by J.E. Bouvier

It was on this tiny remote island that a mysterious being from another dimension provided John with an unbelievably detailed and graphic description of precisely how the world is going to end. Fortunately, this phenomenal insight into the end of the world was recorded by John in manuscripts that were later translated into hundreds of modern languages to warn future generations of the danger. Visitors to Patmos can actually examine the interior of a cave believed to be the home of John during his exile and inspect symbols scribed on the wall that give evidence of his presence and his identity. Some believe John recorded his journey to the future in this cave. However, no one knows for sure where the actual composition of the manuscripts took place since there are many inspirational places on the island.

John "...was banished to Patmos about A.D. 94 and liberated about A.D. 96. Patmos, a barren rocky little island belonging to a group of islands called the Sporades, is ten miles long by five miles... It lies forty miles off the coast of Asia Minor and it was important because it was the last haven on the voyage from Rome to Ephesus and the first in the reverse direction. Banishment to a remote island was a common form of Roman punishment... Such banishment involved the loss of civil rights and all property except enough for a bare existence. People so banished were not personally ill-treated and were not confined in prison on their island but free to move within its narrow limits."[1]

John was held captive by the Romans on Patmos for about two years. After his release from exile he lived the rest of his life in Ephesus where he later died and was buried.

The island of Patmos[2]

BACK TO THE FUTURE

John witnessed a supernatural vision of the events leading up to and including the seven-year-invasion of earth climaxing with Armageddon and the end of the world. In some miraculous manner John was able to experience the entire seven years of the invasion within the two physical years of his exile on Patmos. The strange and powerful messenger apparently had the incredible ability to fast forward the vision of the future at times, thus shortening the total exposure of John to the excruciating impact of the invasion. Clearly this superior being has powers far beyond those of mortal mankind. In addition, the Roman guards on the island apparently didn't notice John's absence as he was routinely and supernaturally transported to and from the future. John likely could only tolerate a limited encounter with the terror in the invasion. Therefore, it's possible that he made numerous trips back to the future, returning to Patmos after each experience to record the amazing events he saw and heard.

We're given limited information about John's life on Patmos but imagine what each of his days may have been like.

Perhaps after a harrowing experience in the future, John returned to Patmos and walked to one of his favorite places that gave him an unobstructed view of the beautiful deep blue Aegean Sea. He situated himself on a rock and concentrated on accurately recording what he had heard and seen in the future. His mind was clear, and there were no distractions. The rhythmic sound of the ocean waves breaking on the rocks beneath him, the fresh smell of salt spray and the cool breeze off the ocean provided a relaxing and peaceful backdrop for his writing.

Although the role John played in recording his encounters with the future was undoubtedly exciting, there was likely another side to his emotions. He witnessed events in a strange world with strange people thousands of years in the future and literally watched helplessly as millions of people suffered and died right in front of him. Then after recording his terrifying experiences John returned to the future again and again to observe the next set of shocking events. Imagine witnessing the death and suffering of so many people and knowing the time for the death of others was just a heartbeat away. If only he could call out and warn them of the impending danger, he could save some of them. He may have even questioned why he was the one to witness such devastating events. However, at some point John likely came to his senses and realized the events he witnessed and recorded were in the distant future and hadn't happened yet. In fact, none of those people actually suffered and died. They would not even be born for thousands of years. John likely recognized that with the help of the very manuscripts he was writing, the people in the targeted generation, whoever they are, could be warned. John's information would surely

39

compel them to discover the way of escape, if they would only heed the warning.

AIR-LIFTED TO SAFETY

Ancient manuscripts reveal a promise made thousands of years ago that a mysterious gift would be sent to earth someday from another dimension giving incredible power beyond the comprehension of mankind to those who discovered and accepted it. As promised, a small package arrived in an obscure town in ancient Israel almost 2,000 years ago unnoticed by most of the world. That amazing gift that has never been fully understood has the extraordinary power to totally transform the lives and alter the futures of those who possess it. I call this priceless, timeless treasure the gift of life! Anyone who possesses the gift will have life that can never be taken away. The key to the secret of this incredible gift has defied understanding by the world's scholars, scientists, doctors and philosophers and remains a baffling mystery to most of the world today.

This astounding gift to humanity frees the recipient from the chains of fear and anxiety, provides hope for the future and reveals the secret to successful living that everyone seeks and desires. This unbelievable gift also provides the key to the secret to surviving the end of the world for those living in the generation targeted by the invasion of planet earth. In fact, those who possess the key to the secret to survival will be the only ones to escape the cataclysmic global invasion. Anyone left will be strongly encouraged to accept the gift of life to escape a fate worse than death, even though they will not be spared the suffering of the devastating attack. Although the gift of life is available to everyone, only those who have *chosen* to accept it will possess its power and become members of a sacred group that I call the "Chosen." These are ordinary people from all walks of life and every part of the world who have discovered and accepted the gift of life.

Before beginning his journey into the future, John was instructed by the supernatural messenger to write letters to seven of the first century congregations of the "Chosen." You can read these letters in what are now the first three chapters of the modern apocalyptic book of the insider information. However, after a detailed description of the letters and their congregations, there is no mention of the "Chosen" living on earth during the invasion. Why? The members of the sacred group who are alive in the "terminal generation" will be mysteriously air-lifted to safety from earth before the invasion begins. Everyone else will be left to suffer the full brunt of the holocaust. I call this bizarre disappearance of people "the great snatch" since the "Chosen" will be taken quickly and without warning. How will people be evacuated from the planet and where will they be taken? What is the key to the secret to surviving the end of the world?

First, discover how the "Chosen" will be removed from earth to safety. Then experience the catastrophic impact the sudden disappearance of hundreds of millions of people will have on the infrastructures of the industrialized nations of the world before the actual invasion begins. Next, examine the recent signs along life's highway that warn the invasion may be dangerously close, perhaps as near as tomorrow's sunrise. Then take a journey with John as he graphically narrates the invasion of earth as seen through his eyes. He will give us the shocking unforgettable details of what will be the world's greatest catastrophe as the curtain comes down on the final act of the drama of humanity. Finally, the ancient manuscripts will reveal the secret of the "Chosen," the final destination of those rescued from earth and the life-saving key to surviving the end of the world.

5

WHERE DID THEY GO?

Several years ago I was anxiously racing to the Los Angeles International Airport to catch an airplane bound for Houston, Texas. Unfortunately, I took a couple of wrong turns on the freeway, had trouble returning the rental car, and ultimately arrived at the terminal five minutes past the scheduled departure time for my flight. I was late, but my flight was also late leaving the gate. I ran to the check-in counter for my flight expecting the attendant to quickly scan the bar code on my boarding pass and usher me to the waiting airplane. However, just as I walked up, she abruptly closed the door to the jet-way in front of me. She stood in front of the door with the determination of a Swiss soldier in the Vatican guarding the Pope. She firmly stated with no remorse, "You're too late for this flight! It's going to leave without you."

Later, I pondered my dilemma and came to the realization it was my fault that I didn't make the flight. There was no mystery. I just didn't leave in time! However, there is a flight we must be prepared to take one day that will provide the only way of escape from the imminent destruction of earth. If we miss that flight to safety, there won't be another!

BEAM ME UP SCOTTY

Since mankind has been clearly warned of the coming invasion some may expect plans for construction of a modern "ark" to be hidden in the ancient manuscripts. Fabrication of such an "escape vehicle(s)" would permit the evacuation of great numbers of people to safety before the world comes to an end. After all, why provide a warning without making a way of escape? Such an ark is fictionalized in the "doomsday" movie *2012*. A set of mammoth boats are designed and fabricated to survive the catastrophic floods and other natural disasters that spell certain doom for earth's inhabitants. To help finance the cost of design and construction of these boats, some seats are sold for such extravagant prices that only the world's wealthiest could afford them. Others are selected to board the boats based solely on their genetic make-up and intrinsic value to repopulating the human race when the floods subside. Of course, seats on the boats are limited and consequently the majority of the world's population is left to die.

The manuscripts with the blueprint for destruction of earth contain no such plans for a twenty-first century ark to save the "terminal generation." However, the manuscripts do indicate that the "Chosen" will be mysteriously evacuated in time to escape annihilation. Who or what is providing the way of escape and if the entire world is destroyed, where will people be taken? Will they go to another planet?

Unlike the movie *2012*, there will be no limit as to how many people will be able to escape by the unorthodox, unimaginable method described in the ancient manuscripts.[1] Believe it or not, this escape to safety will require the

44

supernatural transformation of people to make a gravity-free flight through the heavens.[2] It will be as though each person will have their own mystical "flight suit." The changed people will literally be "snatched" up in the clouds and whisked to a place of safety as though they were drawn by a powerful magnet. Now you may hear the music from the popular epic series *Star Trek* playing in the background as you visualize people on earth calling out to someone above "Beam me up Scotty," but how will this incredible transformation and mass exodus of people from earth be accomplished?

This unexplained metamorphosis of the human bodies will be automatic and instantaneous when it's time to evacuate the planet. Millions, perhaps hundreds of millions, of people who make up the "Chosen" from all over the world will stream toward the stars in a ghostly processional at the exact same moment. Unfortunately, billions more will be left on the earth in utter shock. You probably can't understand how that will happen because it sounds too bizarre to believe. I agree! However, most people don't even understand how the practical products of modern technologies work that we use every day, but that doesn't stop us from using them.

In this case, we're discussing the mind-boggling process for the supernatural alteration of people and their journey that will be provided by a powerful unexplained force from another dimension. That awesome power that will provide the escape from danger is beyond our comprehension and defies all scientific explanation. We must trust the mysterious mode of escape or simply resolve to stay behind and endure the unimaginable horrifying consequences.

TIMING IS EVERYTHING

There will be an ear-piercing sound like a trumpet announcing the time to abandon the doomed planet.[3] If you ever lived in a tornado-prone area like Kansas, you likely have heard the occasional loud drone of a siren warning of an approaching tornado. The sirens that save many lives every year are a warning to immediately seek shelter to escape imminent danger. Similarly, the message of John's manuscripts is sounding the warning siren that the earth is now in the crosshairs of the invasion, and people should be prepared to make their way of escape to safety.

When the sound like a trumpet signals the time to go anyone who doesn't have the key to the secret of escape will be left on earth to live and likely die in the greatest global catastrophe the world has ever experienced. There won't be a countdown from 10 and then lift off! There won't be a delay waiting on stragglers madly rushing to search for the secret to the way of escape. One day when we least expect it, it will just be GO!

In the early days of civilization a man named Noah received advanced information that the world would soon be destroyed by a great flood. Noah was given detailed instructions to build an ark or mammoth boat that would provide a way of escape for him and his family, representatives of the animal kingdom and those that chose to believe Noah's warning. However, the rain didn't begin for more than a hundred years while the ark was in construction and no one took Noah's warning seriously. No one could imagine the possibility of the entire world being flooded. The delay between the warning and the flood fostered a false sense of security, complacency and increased disbelief among the people. Of course, the flood arrived when they least expected it! Noah sailed with only his family and the animals and the rest is history!

Personally, I believe it would have been better to trust Noah and reserve a seat in the ark even if you were not totally convinced the earth would flood. If it never rained a drop, the worst that could have happened is spending a few nights on a big boat in dry dock with a zoo! How bad could that have been?

And if you insisted Noah was wrong and stayed behind, you would pay the penalty for making your point when it did flood. You can only tread water for so long! Timing is everything.

UNIDENTIFIED FLYING OBJECTS

Imagine the following scenario describing what the dramatic worldwide disappearance of people of all ages and all walks of life may be like and how it may be reported to those remaining throughout the world.

All the people "snatched" during the evacuation of the "Chosen" will likely leave their clothes right where they were standing, working, etc. The piles of clothes left in homes, office buildings, buses, trains, etc. will give the appearance that the bodies were literally vaporized by some futuristic alien weapon. The earthlings who rocket into the heavens will have no further use for clothes since they will be given a completely new set of attire more appropriate for the flight to their ultimate destination.

Where did they go?
Photograph by J.E. Bouvier

There are millions of people who are members of the "Chosen" and hold critical positions in government, transportation, the military, utilities, the medical profession and other areas of the infrastructure necessary for everyday life. Therefore, their sudden absence from the workplace at the exact same time on the same day will trigger an unbelievable and disastrous domino effect that will send the planet reeling. Everyone will be frantically searching for an explanation to the crippled infrastructures that can no longer sustain the routine workload for everyday life.

People will be left without basic services. Even the food supply will be interrupted due to the massive number of accidents resulting in snarled traffic on the highways. There will be insufficient labor to load and unload ships, trains, planes and trucks that do arrive at their destination. There will be a lack of fresh water. Electric generating plants and waste treatment facilities will be operating at less than full capacity if operating at all. All of this will serve to heighten the level of panic in the world due to the unexplained disappearance of so many people. Police and emergency crews will suddenly be incapable of responding to the overwhelming number of accident calls, emergencies and missing persons' reports. Martial law will be enforced wherever possible in an attempt to maintain order. Hospitals will find themselves turning away patients because they are understaffed, overworked and filled to capacity with the injured and dying. Fires will burn uncontrollably due to lack of firefighters to extinguish them. Cruise ships at sea, with many of the crew missing, will wander aimlessly with thousands of frightened and hysterical passengers. Trains and subways will run at top speed without the benefit of the engineers at the controls, speeding by scheduled stops and destined for eventual disaster.

Many airports will be closed due to insufficient personnel to staff the control towers. Airplanes flying without pilots will suddenly drop off the radar screens and eventually spiral uncontrollably to the ground as fuel is exhausted. The Air Route Traffic Control Centers (ARTCC) will try in vain to deal with the skies crowded with traffic that ignores their panic stricken instructions to avoid mid-air collisions. On June 1, 2009 the world mourned the loss of 228 people that died unexpectedly when Air France Airlines Flight 447 mysteriously crashed into the Atlantic Ocean shortly after leaving Rio de Janeiro, Brazil bound for Paris, France. Vessels from many nations rallied to search for debris, survivors and the black box that may explain the mystery of the crash. The entire world was on alert anticipating news of survivors. From this strange and unexplained disappearance of a single aircraft, can you imagine the pandemonium that will take place when hundreds, perhaps thousands of commercial as well as private and even military aircraft around the world simultaneously disappear from radar screens?

Television, radio and newspaper reporters will soon be exhausted investigating one plane crash, train wreck, incident in the shipping lanes and vehicle accident after another around the world. Calls will come from every continent, jamming the phone lines with reports of sightings of millions of strange unidentified flying objects (UFOs) streaming into the atmosphere and disappearing into the clouds just before the pandemonium started. Many eyewitnesses will report that the objects had a strange resemblance to ghostly shapes of bodies streaming up to the heavens as though they were being drawn by some kind of powerful supernatural magnet. It will be enough to send chills through those who witness it. Still others may report hearing a loud noise just before the disappearance of the people. The noise may be reported as an earsplitting explosion. Some people may describe hearing a deafening blast that sounded like a horn or trumpet of monstrous acoustic proportions. There is no doubt this will be the sound that signals the evacuation of the "Chosen" to safety.

INVASION OF THE BODY SNATCHERS

The illusion of an alien flying saucer in Piraeus, Greece[4]

The headlines of the papers the morning after the disappearance of the "Chosen" may likely read **"MILLIONS MISSING-WHERE DID THEY GO?"** As the media and leaders of the world attempt to explain what happened, they will be unable to find any correlation between those who were taken and those who were left. The missing people will be from all over the world, but it will seem the United States is the nation most affected. Some of the missing will be rich, some poor, some famous. They will be male and female and from all races and backgrounds. They will range in age from very young to very old. Strangely enough, it will seem that children were a definite target of the invaders since the world will be virtually void of them. The only factor all those taken appear to have in common is that they all vanish at the exact same moment in space. Of course, the actual time of the disappearances in the various time zones will be different.

As the leaders of our nation and the world convene in one televised press conference after another, they will struggle to suggest any reasonable explanation for the mass disappearance of so many people. The U.S. Senate, the House of Representatives and state and local governments will be devastated by missing members, plunging the mammoth political machines into turmoil. The governing bodies of other industrialized nations around the globe will be in a similar predicament. The military will be in a state of confusion with strategic leadership missing and insufficient armed forces personnel to operate the aircraft, warships and other equipment critical to defending the security of our nation. Some high ranking officials left in the government may speculate this is an enormous, carefully orchestrated diabolical terrorist plot. Perhaps their ultimate plan is to render the political infrastructure, leadership and military support of the twenty most industrialized nations (G20) helpless by mysteriously extracting massive numbers of essential people from around the world. They would then be able to successfully execute simultaneous attacks on multiple targets during the chaos.

Before the invasion is launched, a charismatic diplomat with an insidious diabolical connection will emerge from the shadows of unknown politicians, immediately captivate the hearts and minds of everyone and ultimately take control of the planet. The chaos in the world due to the unexplained disappearance of hundreds of millions of people will, in fact, create the perfect environment for this bright aspiring new leader to take the reins and calm a population galvanized with fear. He will reassure the remaining population that all will be well as he makes plans to take the helm of a new worldwide organization. He will likely offer a seemingly plausible explanation for the disappearance of the millions of people and a plan to move forward that will help put the world at ease. In fact, the people left will be presented with a great lie that they will swallow hook, line and sinker. Who will be in a better position to manufacture such deception but this shrewd world ruler of the future? Who is he? Where will he come from?

Although there is no limit to the lies this world leader may offer, imagine the following, very believable scenario of deception. The brilliantly articulate diplomat will suggest that the recent mysterious event is believed to be an invasion of what he calls "the body snatchers." Yes, he is referring to an alien life-form from a distant galaxy with the power to instantaneously beam unsuspecting people up from earth to their spacecrafts. He explains the loud noise heard just before the disappearance of people was the sound of a massive burst of energy that powers the "retractor beam" used to "vacuum up" the humans. He may claim there were hundreds of sightings of strange spacecraft at strategic locations around the world just prior to the disappearance of the masses of people. There will be rumors that the aliens were kidnapping people in random locations to supplement a dwindling food supply on their own planet. Others will speculate that the aliens were benefactors from an advanced civilization in deep space sent to rescue the earthlings from the imminent destruction of earth by nuclear war with plans to start a new civilization on a distant planet. Perhaps they will return for those who were left. In fact, this "self-appointed" messiah of the world may imply this is just the first wave of attacks by the alien life-forms, hypothesizing there will be more to come. Remember, he is talking to a generation that is mesmerized by theories of alien-invaders, UFO's, and the possibility of intelligent life on other planets.

If it seems like a bizarre, unlikely scenario that people will have difficulty swallowing, consider the actual dramatization of the conquest of earth by alien invaders in 1938. Orson Welles, working for the Columbia Broadcasting System, produced and broadcasted a fictionalized drama on the radio of an H.G. Wells classic science fiction novel, *"The War of the Worlds."* As the radio station beamed the dramatically realistic account across America the day before Halloween, Americans everywhere were convinced they were being invaded by Martians. The consequences were devastating, and there was nationwide panic. Some people were even killed in the chaos and confusion. Do I think people will believe a story about alien invaders to explain the disappearance of millions of people in a world bursting at the seams with panic and chaos? Absolutely!

Now before examining the graphic details of the invasion leading to Armageddon and the end of the world, we must turn back the clock again and visit with a man whose life was abruptly interrupted when he was kidnapped from his home as a young boy. The boy grew to manhood and led a miraculously successful life in captivity. He rose to political stardom in the court of his enemy and became the recipient of mysterious information from beyond our world that complements the information given to John on Patmos 600 years later.

6

"THE DOOMSDAY CLOCK"

*M*ore than 600 hundred years before John received the insider information a mysterious messenger from another dimension appeared on earth and revealed a supernatural clock (foretelling the timing of future events) to a man named Daniel who lived in ancient Babylon. The face of the clock had only three future occurrences scribed on it, but each event had immense significance to Israel and the world. That clock, left hanging by the messenger in the universal expanse of timeless space until today, came to life and started ticking shortly after the timing of the events was explained to Daniel. As the clock ticked off about five hundred years, the first two events occurred precisely as described and then the clock abruptly stopped as suddenly as it started. However, once the clock is set in motion again, it will begin counting down the days the human race has remaining on earth until the end of the world. The messenger was describing the shocking "Doomsday Clock" for mankind. What will trigger this mysterious clock currently frozen in time to begin ticking again? Exactly how much time does the human race have before they are destroyed, once it is activated again?

CLUES

The present day literary volume containing the insider information, the description of the "Doomsday Clock," and the key to the secret to surviving the end of the world is a collection of ancient manuscripts translated from the original Hebrew, Greek and Aramaic into hundreds of modern languages. Imbedded in the numerous accounts of historical significance, principles for living and mysteries of the unknown are countless clues, milestones and signs to help us understand more about the coming invasion of earth and the identity of the generation targeted for destruction. The good news is the meaning of the clues and encoded passages describing the future are not buried in the sands of ancient Egyptian tombs or scribed in mysterious hieroglyphics requiring intricate codes for deciphering as fictionalized in movies. Although shrouded in the unknown, the mystery of the clues can be understood by simply studying the translations of the ancient manuscripts and looking carefully at events unfolding in the world around us.

The mysterious Sphinx, pyramids and tombs near Cairo, Egypt
Photograph by J.E. Bouvier

Therefore, before we depart for the future with John to experience the horror of the invasion and the battle of Armageddon, it will be helpful to obtain some important background information and discover clues to the timing of events that will precede the end of the world. The next few chapters will provide the following:

- An understanding of the exact amount of time mankind has remaining to the end of the world once the "Doomsday Clock" is activated again.

- The circumstances and world affairs surrounding an earthshaking event that will set the "Doomsday Clock" in motion and start it ticking again.

- The origin and personal characteristics of the most notorious world dictator in history that may surface soon and rule the world during the coming invasion.

- A description of the one-world government that will provide the political platform for the modern dictator to assume possession of the planet.

- Signs of the beginning of the end of the world.

- Information about technology required for events predicted to occur during the invasion that is commercially available today for the first time in history.

KIDNAPPED

Daniel was a young Jewish boy whose home was in Jerusalem in ancient Israel. In approximately 600 B.C. the city of Jerusalem was besieged and pillaged by the armies of King Nebuchadnezzar of Babylon resulting in many of the city's inhabitants taken captive. Young Daniel, as well as three of his friends, were among the boys chosen by the representatives of the king to be worthy for training in Nebuchadnezzar's personal court. Can you imagine what these four young children experienced having been kidnapped, separated from their family and friends and taken captive to a foreign land across the desert hundreds of miles from home? Little did Daniel's parents know that the secrets of the "Doomsday Clock," as well as clues to the mystery of the world's most notorious future dictator and his government, would be revealed to their son by strange messengers from another dimension of the universe.

> *Sometimes events take place in our lives or the lives of our loved ones, like the abduction of Daniel and his friends that are unexplainable and absolutely unbearable. How could this kidnapping happen to an innocent child and to his family? We may even blame God for things we don't understand and, at least in our own minds, we don't deserve.*

Daniel was the kind of boy any of us would be proud to have as a son. He was intelligent and wise beyond his years. This bright student apparently had good study habits and was extremely knowledgeable in many subjects, including science. He appeared to have an uncanny ability to discern right from wrong at a young age and made decisions carefully and wisely. More importantly, he would later prove the value of his Israelite training in the Babylonian royal court.

Daniel and his three friends made the best of their captivity in Babylon. In fact, there is no record that they ever complained about their strange new surroundings, even under adverse conditions. They immediately found favor with Nebuchadnezzar. The king found Daniel to be far superior in matters of wisdom and understanding than all Nebuchadnezzar's magicians and astrologers. In addition, Daniel had an amazing ability to interpret dreams, which he used to help the king understand visions when others in the king's court failed to do so. As a result, the king rewarded Daniel by making him ruler of the entire province of Babylon, a position second only in rank to the king. Daniel was respected and rewarded for interpreting dreams for subsequent rulers and continued to have a place of prominence in Babylon, even after the overthrow of the Babylonian Empire by the Medo-Persians.

FROZEN IN TIME

Daniel had risen to a place of prominence in the land of his captors but was lonesome for his home. The city of Jerusalem had been completely destroyed and the Jewish Temple obliterated by Nebuchadnezzar in approximately 586 B.C. Daniel was anxious to know when Jerusalem and the Temple would be rebuilt and when his people could return to their homes. One night while Daniel was meditating and searching for answers to this very question, a supernatural messenger from another dimension descended to earth and physically touched him to get his attention. This strange visitor to earth revealed a mystical clock to Daniel with the timing of three specific future events.[1]

While the first two occurrences provided incredible insight to Daniel and the Jews living in captivity, the last event will mark the beginning of the end for the generation of people in the world targeted for destruction by the invasion of earth. Little did Daniel know that the strange messenger was describing a "Doomsday Clock" for the "terminal generation" of the human race. Unfortunately, the timing of the events appeared to be in some kind of code. This clock was described having a total of seventy weeks of time for mankind until the end of the world, but we must explore the manuscripts further to decode the meaning of the seventy weeks.

The messenger explained that the first event on the clock was the rebuilding of Jerusalem, which would be completed exactly seven weeks after the Jewish captives were allowed to return to their homes in Jerusalem. At this point Daniel had the answer to his burning question. He had only to wait for the king to announce that the Jews were free to return home and work could begin on the city, but how long is seven weeks?

The messenger continued his explanation to Daniel that precisely sixty-two weeks after the city of Jerusalem is rebuilt Jesus, the long-awaited Messiah promised to Israel in the ancient manuscripts, will begin his public ministry and then later be executed. Daniel was familiar with this ancient prediction. The strange visitor then explained that the rebuilt city of Jerusalem and the Temple described in the first event will be destroyed again. The messenger elaborated that the civilization responsible for the destruction of Jerusalem this time will also produce the bloodline of a man who will become a future world leader and initiate the third event which will activate the "Doomsday Clock" again. In other words, we know the heritage of this future ruler simply by observing which civilization destroyed Jerusalem sometime after Jesus was executed.

Of course, after the explanation of the timing of the first two events, Daniel had no idea what the messenger was talking about since the third event would not occur for thousands of years. This message is for us! The total accumulated time on the clock for the first two events was sixty-nine weeks so there is still one missing week. Daniel's messenger explained that the third event on the clock is a covenant or peace treaty that the future world ruler will negotiate with Israel lasting one week, which accounts for the missing one. Why is the treaty with Israel important to us? We will see that the signing of this treaty is the event that will actually trigger the "Doomsday Clock" and initiate the deadly invasion of our planet. The clock will begin counting down the time remaining before the complete destruction of the human race and it could be activated any day! Once the clock is set in motion, nothing can slow it down or stop it!

This treaty with Israel will be an earth-shattering event. Israel has been at war much of the time since becoming a nation again in 1948. Even today, her Muslim neighbors in Iran are determined to totally annihilate the nation of Israel and her allies and have announced their intention to the world more than once. As recently as June 2010, Israel approached the precipice of war as a result of activities associated with the maritime blockade of ports on the Gaza Strip put in place by Israel in 2007. Most of the world condemned Israel for boarding and inspecting ships loaded with relief supplies bound for the Gaza Strip. Israel was only trying to stop the flow of weapons en route to Hamas terrorists who had been relentlessly lobbing rockets as far into the interior of Israel as possible. Even the current (2009) administration of the United States has failed to openly support Israel as Iran threatens to become involved in breaking the blockade.

It seems likely that Israel will welcome a peace treaty with a strong ally, and the new world ruler will be poised and ready to oblige her. However, since the word of the world ruler will be like ice melting in the desert heat, the messenger was quick to add that the ruler will break the treaty with Israel near the mid-point of the terms of the treaty. There is no timetable given for the negotiation of the peace treaty with Israel and, as of 2010, it has not yet taken place. Therefore, there is a gap in the timeline between the time of Jesus and the signing of the treaty with Israel. Fortunately, the "Doomsday Clock" has been frozen in time for more than two thousand years, delaying the end of the world.

From the above "riddle" we know the following:

•	The time to restore and rebuild Jerusalem	7 weeks
•	The time from the rebuilding of Jerusalem until the time of Jesus (the Messiah)	62 weeks
	The gap in time where the world is today	
•	The term of the treaty (covenant) with Israel	1 week

Total time on the "Doomsday Clock"	70 weeks

DECODING THE TIMELINE

Decoding the timeline on the "Doomsday Clock" requires a closer study of the ancient manuscripts. According to Stephen Miller, "The sevens are literal seven-year periods totaling 490 years."[2] Therefore, one week is simply seven years. Although there are many different opinions as to when the 490 years begin, it seems there is only one view that precisely conforms to the predictions given by the messenger, agrees with accounts in the ancient manuscripts and is consistent with historical evidence. Artaxerxes I King of Persia gave a decree to the prophet Ezra in 458 B.C. to rebuild the Temple and the city of Jerusalem that had been destroyed by the Babylonians in 586 B.C. Therefore, "...the decree to Ezra in 458 B.C. is the correct starting point for the seventy sevens, but a survey of the events contained in the first sixty-nine sevens is necessary to demonstrate the appropriateness of this option… If this view is correct, 483 years after 458 B.C. would result in a date of A.D. 26, the time when many scholars believe Christ was baptized and began his public ministry as the Messiah. Jesus' anointing for ministry came at his baptism; thus he became the 'Anointed One' at that time, an amazing fulfillment of prophecy."[3] The "Doomsday Clock" was set in motion and started the countdown in 458 B.C. when the king of Persia gave Ezra the decree that permitted the Jewish people to return to Jerusalem. The amazing accuracy of these predictions gives us confidence that the warning of Armageddon and the end of the world must be seriously embraced by our generation!

Now, we know the time on the "Doomsday Clock" in terms we understand.

• The time to rebuild Jerusalem	7 weeks or 49 years
• The time from the end of the 49 years until the time of Jesus (the Messiah the Prince) The gap in time where the world is today	62 weeks or 434 years
• The term of the treaty (covenant) with Israel	1 week or 7 years
Total time on the "Doomsday Clock" when described	70 weeks or 490 years
Total time remaining on the "Doomsday Clock"	1 week or **7 years**

"In A.D. 70 Titus Vespasianus led the Roman legions against Jerusalem and utterly destroyed both the city and the temple."[4] Therefore, almost 600 years after Daniel recorded the predictions of the messenger the city of Jerusalem was destroyed by the powerful Roman Empire. As a result, the Jews were dispersed throughout the world. This event also establishes the fact that the bloodline of the world ruler will be out of the nations and people who made up the powerful ancient Roman Empire.

Seven literal years remain on the "Doomsday Clock." Therefore, seven years is the length of time Israel will be promised protection from her enemies with a covenant or peace treaty negotiated by the world ruler just prior to the beginning of the invasion. The signing of the infamous treaty with Israel will provide the trigger starting the "Doomsday Clock" and the imminent invasion of earth. Since there are only seven years left on the "Doomsday Clock," seven years must also be the exact duration of the invasion of earth climaxing with Armageddon, but why did the clock stop? There can only be one answer.

When the clock starts ticking again, mankind will be subjected to the longest seven years of pain, suffering and death in the history of the world. As long as the "Doomsday Clock" is frozen in time each generation has an opportunity to understand the warning in the ancient manuscripts and to accept the gift of life. Thus they can avoid the annihilation of mankind and the end of the world should they be living in the generation targeted for destruction-the "terminal generation." How much time does the human race have remaining on earth before Armageddon? We only know that every sunrise brings the event that will activate the clock one day closer.

REFLECTIONS

- The mysterious "Doomsday Clock" was described to Daniel with a total of 490 years.

- The clock started ticking with the decree from the King of Persia to Ezra in 458 B.C. to rebuild Jerusalem.

- The clock stopped ticking about A.D. 26. There is currently a gap in time of almost 2,000 years in which the clock has been silent and frozen in time.

- After the destruction of Jerusalem in A.D. 70 by the Romans, the Jewish people were dispersed throughout the world.

- The destruction of Jerusalem by the Romans in A.D. 70 establishes the ancestry of the one who will rule during the invasion of earth. His bloodline will come out of the people and nations of the powerful ancient Roman Empire.

- Once the treaty for peace is signed with Israel by the modern world ruler, the "Doomsday Clock" will be activated and the invasion of planet earth will be initiated. The human race will have precisely seven years until the end of the world.

Explore the unique character of the world ruler who is destined to become a brutal dictator and examine the twenty-first century government which will provide the political springboard for him to begin his rule.

7

HE WILL RULE
THE WORLD

The chaos, pain, suffering and death accompanying the invasion of earth and climaxing with Armageddon will be unprecedented. However, the messengers who described the "Doomsday Clock" to Daniel also provided a graphic picture of the man who will compound the horror of the invasion by ruling the world with an "iron fist." Daniel received this incredible insight more than 600 years before the insider information was given to John on the island of Patmos. This charismatic politician and dictator of the future will likely promise the world real change, prosperity, transparency and unparalleled fundamental political and financial reform to achieve his covert agenda. Sounds good, doesn't it? Learn about this future world ruler, his new world government and the secret weapon he will use to seduce the world's population while quietly taking complete control of the planet.

The time is drawing near for this unknown diplomat to emerge from the shadows and assume his role of leadership and responsibility in one of the newest, fastest growing world governments in history. The birth and growth of this political infrastructure appears to be fulfilling a prediction made by Daniel more than two thousand years ago and is one of the last major signposts on the road to the beginning of the end of the world. An understanding of the structure and diplomatic philosophy of this new government is critical to gauging how close we are to the beginning of the end, and we are dangerously close!

NATIONS THAT DOMINATE THE WORLD

Daniel quickly rose to stardom in Babylon by interpreting dreams for the kings he served, but one day Daniel had a dream of his own. He carefully recorded the interpretation of the vision with the help of strange visitors from another dimension who had a supernatural knowledge of the future. This vision, given to him by a power beyond mortal man described empires that have ruled the world in the past and predicted the next one that will rule the world in the future. It began with the powerful empire of Babylon and climaxed with a modern world government that will be ruled by the most brutal dictator in all history. However, the dream was cloaked in mysterious symbols, code words and descriptions of weird animals that made it difficult for Daniel to understand. Fortunately, the interpretation of the dream by the mysterious messenger makes the meaning of the dream possible to comprehend.

Why is it important to understand an ancient dream about mystifying animals and world governments in the past? This dream holds the clues to the identity of the modern government of the dictator who will rule the apocalyptic world as it plunges to a dramatic cataclysmic conclusion.

Daniel saw four strange looking animals in the dream that can be characterized as follows:

- A lion that had the wings of an eagle which were later plucked as the lion stood upon his feet like a man with a man's heart.

- A bear that rose up on one side and had three ribs between his teeth.

- A leopard that had four wings and four heads.

- A fourth beast that had great iron teeth and ten horns. Then there came up among the ten horns another little horn which jerked out three of the previous horns by the roots. This little horn had eyes like a man and a mouth speaking great things.

Daniel was troubled by the bizarre-looking animals in the vision and didn't understand the significance of them. He asked one of the messengers to explain the meaning of the four animals. The explanation was given that the four beasts are four kings or world empires that rule the world. The animals in the dream are actually symbols or code words which are uniquely representative of the kingdoms or nations and their leaders. Scholars who are familiar with the history of these nations and what they stood for have no problem recognizing them from the code words. For example, what nation today is symbolized by the powerful eagle? Of course, it's the symbol or code word for the United States.

The following is an interpretation of the code words for the first three animals or beasts symbolizing nations that ruled the world in sequence starting with the one most familiar to Daniel.

"The first animal resembled a lion; however, this was an unusual-looking lion because it had large wings, like those of an eagle… A number of factors demonstrate that the lion and eagle are apt symbols of Babylon."[1] The coded message goes further to explain historical facts about Nebuchadnezzar, the king of Babylon. "The lion's wings being torn off speaks of the king's insanity and loss of power; standing on two feet like a man and receiving a human heart (mind) denotes Nebuchadnezzar's humanitarian rule after his insanity; …"[2]

A second beast appeared in the vision. "Medo-Persia followed Babylon as the next great world empire, and the bear was an apt symbol of that kingdom, which was noted for its great size and fierceness in battle."[3] Daniel also had some familiarity with the second animal. "The bear 'had three ribs in its mouth,' which may safely be understood to represent the conquests of the empire."[4] Most scholars interpret these three conquests by Medo-Persia to be Babylon, Lydia and Egypt.

"The third animal resembled a 'leopard' but it was a very strange looking leopard. Four wings like those of a bird were upon its back (or sides), and it had four heads. Following Medo-Persia, Greece dominated the world. Greece is aptly represented by this flying leopard, for its conquests were carried out with lightning speed, and it had an insatiable lust for territory. Alexander the Great invaded Asia Minor in 334 B.C. and within ten short years (by the age of thirty-two) had conquered the entire Medo-Persian Empire to the borders of India."[5]

The explanation of these three animals was interesting, but Daniel was especially fascinated by the fourth beast because it was uniquely different from all the others. It had large, ferocious-looking teeth of iron in its mouth and ten horns on its head. "By the second century B.C., Rome had superseded Greece as the dominant world power. The fourth beast, therefore, represents the Roman Empire... Rome possessed a power and longevity unlike anything the world had ever known. Nations were crushed under the iron boot of the Roman legions, its power was virtually irresistible and the extent of its influence surpassed the other three kingdoms."[6] Since the fourth beast is symbolic of Rome, "... the ten horns coming out of the fourth beast represent a confederation of kings (kingdoms or nations) that emanate from the old Roman Empire."[7] After the fall of the Roman Empire there is a gap of more than 1,500 years before the next world power emerges.

THE LITTLE HORN

While Daniel was pondering the ten horns coming out of the head of the fourth beast, he noticed another little horn coming up among them. This little horn or ruler is small at first and very different from the others. However, he will rapidly gain strength. Based on the explanation from the messenger, Daniel predicted that "... the ruler (little horn) of this coalition (ten horns) will be brilliant (eyes like a man) and arrogant (mouth speaking arrogant things). He will conquer three kingdoms (or nations) that will resist him and thereby gain firm control over the whole empire."[8] In other words, he will be the ruler or dictator of the new world government made up of a coalition of nations with his roots or ancestry in the nations and people of the powerful ancient Roman Empire. While boasting of his profound, heartfelt desire to serve the people and redistribute the wealth of the world to improve the standard of living for everyone in the face of global turmoil, he will secretly be anti-good, anti-others and anti-God. We will call him the Antichrist.

HOW WILL HE DO IT?

It would seem virtually impossible in this day and time that a single individual could rise to power undetected by the vigilant radar of the sophisticated intelligence-gathering systems of the world's most powerful industrialized nations and successfully take control of the planet. How will he do it? Think about the conditions that would have to exist in order for this relatively unknown diplomat to emerge from the shadows and skyrocket to power unchallenged by most of the world.

1. He must have the profile, personality and charisma of a born leader that will allow him to rapidly gain support of the population and heads of state alike.

2. An international infrastructure or world government rooted in the ancient Roman Empire must be born to embrace the Antichrist and give him a political springboard to launch his conquest of the world.

3. The idea and initial use of a global currency must be introduced to provide the first step in establishing a new, cashless world financial infrastructure necessary to control the world.

4. The world must be in such a position that the Antichrist can manipulate it.

1. PROFILE OF A WORLD RULER

First, what characteristics and personality must the Antichrist possess to reach and maintain the powerful position of authority necessary to rule the entire modern-day world? Using the traits of successful world leaders of the past and present as models, supplemented by clues found in the ancient manuscripts, we can paint an accurate picture of the dictator anyone will be able to recognize.

- The relatively unknown diplomat will arrive on the political scene armed with robust connections to a network of powerful conspirators whose tireless energy will fuel his meteoric rise to power and suppress any challengers.

- This tyrant of the future will have a physical appearance of a distinguished respected individual, a great statesman and a born leader. He will likely be tall, lean and handsome as have been many of our own great leaders in the United States.

- This man will be well-educated, respected by all and grounded in politics, international finance and economics. He will likely graduate from one of the world's finest institutions of higher learning. This statesman will be able to articulate plans and solutions to all of the world's problems in a way unparalleled by his predecessors.

- The epitome of evil disguised as a polished politician will appear to have a genuine passion to stabilize the economy of the world following the unexplained disappearance of so many people. He will have the popularity of a rock star and attract throngs of people wherever he goes.

- The popular new "left wing" diplomat who offers the world revolutionary change will have the support and praise of the liberal media. They will embrace his ideas, build on his strengths, and refuse to disclose or even discuss his vague background or any of his shortcomings, weaknesses or mistakes. The media will believe his every word looking for a promising, noteworthy phrase to tell the world. This man can do no wrong.

- This dictator of the modern world will have an unparalleled, ever-present arrogant composure and a swagger in his walk that constantly boasts of his egotistical, overwhelming self-confidence. He will fear nothing and no one.

- The shrewd politician will possess a charismatic personality that will attract the population of the world and heads of state to his ideals like a magnet. His vision will appeal equally to the heads of the largest industrialized nations and dictators of rogue countries.

- The secret weapon of the Antichrist will be a policy of deceit and seduction. He will destroy others by subtle, peaceful means.[9]

- This charismatic diplomat will have the stamina, ruthlessness and ability of Stalin, Hitler and other dictators to eliminate without remorse those who stand in his way.

- With his birthright in the ancient, powerful Roman Empire, this modern dictator will have the mind of a brilliant military strategist. He will conquer, rule and maintain order in the world, boasting of an arsenal of weapons of mass destruction at his disposal but never actually having to use them.[10]

- This political organizer will successfully execute amazing acts of diplomacy promoting world peace, security, economic stability and prosperity. He will quickly attract and hold the popular vote of people worldwide and lure a strong following of all nationalities.

- This cunning politician will seduce leaders of the most powerful nations of the world to voluntarily give up their power to the Antichrist.[11]

- In a day when most frontrunners in politics are fearful to publicly identify themselves with any religious belief, the Antichrist will give the appearance of supporting the popular ecumenical religious movement better known as the one-world religion. The Antichrist, "… will give tacit approval to the ecumenical church, not because he believes in it, but because of its tremendous political overtones and his aspiration to control the world. He apparently will be dominated by the ecumenical church… But this will all be subterfuge on his part until he can gather sufficient control to throw her off and kill this idolatrous ecumenical religion that is gathering momentum in our own generation."[12] The Antichrist will tolerate this religious movement until about the mid-point of the invasion. Then he will destroy the competing religious faction and create his own mandated religion, the worship of the Antichrist.

- Ultimately, it will be revealed that this extraordinary statesman has a diabolical umbilical cord to the cold-blooded demonic power of Satan himself, the prince of darkness.[13]

- The Antichrist will lie, blaspheme and curse God, use the power of Satan to further his cause, take control over the world's finances and attempt to destroy those who obtain the gift of life after the evacuation of the "Chosen."[14]

This diabolical Trojan horse of the twenty-first century will be gracefully invited into the living rooms of the world's population as well as the secure offices of the heads of state before they realize the formidable danger that's concealed within.

Do you think you will recognize him? Do you know him or have you seen him? He may very well be on the scene somewhere in the world today. Of course, he will be waiting in the shadows to make his move to the position being prepared for him.

2. THE PHOENIX OF THE ROMAN EMPIRE

The powerful Antichrist will require a new world government with the political infrastructure and global influence that can successfully launch his career as a world dictator. This new world government described by Daniel will emerge like the mythical Phoenix bird from the ashes of the ancient Roman Empire. Now discover how a government recently born in the twentieth century against all odds may satisfy the following requirements and fulfill the prophecy of a new world government that has been "on hold" for more than two thousand years. To fulfill the prophecy the global government must:

- Consist of a federation of European nations with their roots in territories once occupied by the ancient Roman Empire.

- Satisfy the prophecy of "ten kings" or kingdoms (nations).

- Embrace a foreign policy of diplomacy and peace rather than military strength.

- Have the promise of becoming a global economic superpower.

EUROPEAN NATIONS ROOTED IN THE ROMAN EMPIRE

Prior to 1951, there was little promise that a federation of European nations born out of the ancient Roman Empire could ever emerge to bring the prophecy of a new world government into reality. With the European nations having more than twenty different languages, closed borders requiring passports to cross from the border of one country to another, dozens of currencies, and past involvement in two World Wars, there was no motivation to unite. However, with the end of World War II, European nations found they had a solid mission to:

- Live in peace and avoid involvement in future world wars.

- Improve their standard of living.

- Begin the reconstruction of Europe which had been ravaged by two world wars. This re-construction could obviously be better facilitated by a federation of the European nations to synergistically finance and accelerate the restoration effort.

In March 1957, the Treaty of Rome was signed with six European countries creating the European Economic Community. This union was formed based on a single market where there would be freedom of movement of goods, services, capital and people. From 1957 until 1973 membership increased to nine member nations and what became the European Union looked like it would soon be the ten nation federation of the Roman Empire fulfilling the prophecy of Daniel. The Treaty of Rome was even signed in Rome and the number of member nations was close to ten. It appeared the plan was coming together and the Phoenix was ready to take flight. In fact, in 1981 the number of nations in the European Union grew to ten. Believing the ancient prediction was fulfilled, many mistakenly began to look for the beginning of the end. However, this was not yet the time. As a matter of fact, in 1990 there were fifteen members in the European Union and in 2004 there were twenty five members. Today there are twenty seven members with additional members pending. However, the member nations must have the correct heritage and the prophecy of the "ten kings" must be satisfied to fulfill the prediction of the next world power.

SATISFY THE PROPHECY OF "TEN KINGS"

The organization of the European Union as a world power is rapidly evolving and any conclusion we make today may have to be adjusted tomorrow. Since the number of member nations in the European Union now exceeds ten we know there is more to the prophecy than just a federation of ten member nations. For example, some nations may have to leave the European Union (EU) and others enter in order for the ten nations in the federation to have the ancient Roman Empire as their true ancestry. The ten kings may even refer to an organization set up worldwide after the Antichrist comes into power dividing the world into ten regions, with each region headed by the leader of one of the ten nations with the correct Roman ancestry. If this is true, there is absolutely nothing to prevent the Antichrist from emerging today from the shadows of politicians and begin his advancement to power.

EMBRACE DIPLOMACY AND PEACE

The Antichrist's weapon of choice for control of the world will be peaceful political diplomacy coupled with deception and seduction.[15] Therefore, the infrastructure that provides the Antichrist the position for world leadership will be expected to adopt an anti-military soft political diplomacy before his introduction to the world. An infrastructure that embraces peaceful diplomacy rather than military power will make the transition to the leadership of the Antichrist in the European Union (EU) almost seamless.

In fact, "While there is no questioning the American superiority in the field of military power (the United States spends more on defense every year than the next ten countries combined) an issue often overlooked in the debate about the global role of the EU is the question of 'soft power.'"[16] Although they do not have the military resources, organization or influence to launch an effective military campaign, the EU has become "… adept at using soft power in its dealings with other countries. In a world in which violence is increasingly rejected as a tool of statecraft (at least among wealthy liberal democracies), the use of diplomacy, political influence, and the pressures of economic competition may be giving the EU a strategic advantage which reduces the need to develop a significant common military capacity."[17] The new economic power of the EU combined with growing alarm at historical US foreign policy based on military might and a growing rejection of US global leadership suggests that a new role was about to be forced on the Europeans… It may be that Europe becomes more adept at using soft power and at building on its political, economic, and diplomatic advantages as an alternative to the increasingly discredited policies of the United States.[18]

The European Union is unknowingly positioning itself for the transition to power by the Antichrist using the weapons of deception and peaceful diplomacy. His fundamental political platform will be to promise peace and security for everyone and eliminate the threat of war. As a matter of fact, even the President of the United States has embraced a shift in United States foreign policy to peaceful political diplomacy. In September 2009 it was reported that "President Barack Obama has decided to scrap plans for a U.S. missile defense shield in the Czech Republic and Poland that had deeply angered Russia, the Czech prime minister confirmed Thursday. NATO's new chief hailed the move as a 'positive step' and a Russian analyst said Obama's decision will increase the chances that Russia will cooperate with the United States in the dispute over Iran's nuclear program"[19] The United States sacrificed the installation of the missile defense shield in exchange for Russia's vague promise of cooperation to enact sanctions on Iran to discourage the development of nuclear weapons. Less than a month later, it was reported that "Russian Prime Minister Vladimir Putin criticized talk of sanctions against Iran on Wednesday undermining U.S. efforts to present a unified front against Tehran's nuclear program at a crucial moment. Putin's comments in China came a day after Russia's foreign minister, at Hillary Rodham Clinton's side in Moscow, said threatening sanctions was 'counterproductive.'"[20] The efforts to befriend Russia only further threatened our national security.

As a candidate for the presidency of the United States, Barack Obama telegraphed to our enemies that he intended to pursue diplomacy without preconditions if he was elected. The United States is certainly doing its part under the current administration to prepare to embrace the peaceful diplomatic policies of the Antichrist when he arrives and eliminate the United States as one of the biggest potential deterrents to his takeover of the world!

THE PROMISE OF A WORLD ECONOMIC SUPER POWER

The infrastructure of Roman origin that the Antichrist will use to launch his world dictatorship must evolve into a world superpower to be effective. The European Union (EU) is quietly gaining political and economic strength each year as the membership continues to increase from the original six members in 1957 to the current twenty seven members with other nations pending. In 2004 the population of the European Union passed that of the United States with more than 450 million people. "While the prospects of the EU becoming a major military power are uncertain, there are no doubts at all about its new status as an economic superpower. The common external tariff is in place, the single market is complete, most of the western member states have adopted a single currency, the Commission has powers to represent the governments of all the member states in negotiations on global trade, and it is now well understood by everyone that the EU is the most powerful actor in those negotiations... With just over 7 percent of the world's population, the European Union accounts for more than 28% of the world's GDP (more even than the United States). It also accounts for more than one-third of global merchandise trade (nearly three times the share of the United States)."[21] GDP or Gross Domestic Product is a measure of the economic performance of a nation. Therefore, in an unprecedented brief fifty year period since the inception of the government, the European Union has already taken its place among the United States, China and Japan as a world economic superpower in its own right.

It appears that the European Union is destined to grow larger, stronger and more politically powerful as time goes on, providing the perfect platform for the Antichrist to launch his stranglehold on the world. "For these reasons-historical precedent, economic growth, and the declining credibility of the US role in the world-the European Union has the opportunity to exert itself as a superpower. Building on the foundation of a different set of values, it can offer a different set of analyses of international problems, a different set of solutions, and an approach to international relations based more on diplomacy and multilateralism."[22] Of course, the strength of the European Union is being tested in 2010 as member nations like Greece, Spain and Italy teeter on the brink of bankruptcy due to unsustainable spending and unprecedented debt.

3. A GLOBAL CURRENCY

One of the last things that will make the peaceful takeover of the world and control of the movement of goods and services possible by the Antichrist is a cashless global financial system. However, it's expected this structure will emerge in several steps that will be palatable to world leaders. The first step is the introduction of a global currency. This currency may emanate from within the very government that the Antichrist will rule. For many years now, the leading currency in the world for financial and commerce matters has been the United States dollar followed by the yen and several other currencies.

"Meanwhile the EU took a dramatic step forward on the economic front in early 2002, with the final adoption of the single currency. A decision had been taken in 1995 to call it the euro, and the timetable agreed under Maastricht required participating states to fix their exchange rate in January 1999... For the first time since the Roman era, most of Europe had a common currency."[23]

"The freedoms of the new Europe have been underpinned-at least in 12 of the member states-by the adoption of the euro, which has not only made it easier for goods and services to cross international boundaries, but has given the EU a world class currency that stands alongside the US dollar, giving the EU a new level of influence over international economic and monetary policies."[24] However, the world has become disenchanted with the United States currency following the 2008 meltdown of the U.S. and world financial markets. The massive spending programs by the United States in 2009-2010, intended to stimulate the economy and rescue the ailing financial, housing, real estate and job markets are expected to contribute to an unprecedented national debt exceeding thirteen trillion dollars in the next few years. This debt unparalleled in history will further weaken and devalue the American dollar and may cause hyper-inflation. As a result, several major industrialized nations are now demanding an alternative currency to replace the dollar in the global financial markets.

In March 2009, "China's central bank has called for the creation of a <u>new global currency</u> as an alternative to the dollar, in the latest sign of that country's growing assertiveness on the international stage. As the U.S. government ramps up spending to stimulate the economy and assist the battered financial sector, Chinese officials are worried that inflation will result-and that would erode the value of their dollar holdings, economists said. 'They would dearly like to tear themselves away from the embrace of the U.S.,' said Eswar Prasad, an economics professor at Cornell University. China's proposal would greatly expand the use of an obscure type of currency created by the International Monetary Fund in 1969 known as 'special drawing rights,' or SDRs. The SDR was originally pegged to the dollar but is now based on the value of four different currencies."[25]

Other countries like Venezuela and the twelve members of the Organization of Petroleum Exporting Countries (OPEC) are courting a global currency backed by oil, a so-called "petro-currency." OPEC includes Iran, Libya and Iraq. Needless to say, a global currency is rapidly gaining momentum. A global currency is the last nail in the coffin for hard currency based financial systems. Next, a single total cashless electronic world financial system will emerge. The world is currently well on its way to a cashless, paperless, electronic infrastructure; it's just a matter of time.

4. THE FRUIT WILL BE RIPE

The world will experience widespread devastation, panic and confusion following the unexplained disappearance of hundreds of millions of people with the evacuation of the "Chosen." The world's leaders will be searching for someone capable of restoring global order and orchestrating the reconstruction of the fractured infrastructures in transportation, commerce, communication, finance, and other critical areas of government and private industry. It's often the case that a new leader is welcomed onto the political stage when a nation is experiencing a crisis. A good example is the 2008 presidential election in the United States. The victorious candidate benefited greatly from the financial crisis engulfing the nation as he promised to save the country from financial catastrophe.

The world will be ready and willing to embrace a strong, energetic, politically correct, charismatic diplomat with the "perfect plan" for restoration of a world in crisis. The Antichrist will be poised to accept that role of responsibility. By this time, he will have attained a position of prominence and respect in the European Union as well as with many of the world leaders, including the United States. He may seduce the world's leaders into creating a New World Order to deal with the global chaos.

This worldwide crisis will also provide the Antichrist the perfect opportunity to establish the global systems necessary for his control of the world. In fact, the massive collapse of world financial markets in 2008 has already set the stage for sweeping changes to be made to the financial markets on a global basis. For the first time in history, "global" seems to be the new buzz word of the industrialized nations. The restructuring of these failed financial systems may, in fact, lay the groundwork for the Antichrist to finish his work with the full cooperation of the world's leaders. The world will be ready for the Antichrist, and he will be ready for the world.

REFLECTIONS

- There is a new, strong federation of 27 European nations called the European Union that emerged from the ashes of the nations of the powerful ancient Roman Empire. All that is left to completely fulfill the prophecy is for the leaders of ten nations (with the correct Roman ancestry), to emerge within the structure of that government. The world may even be divided into ten regions under those leaders.

- The Antichrist will be a direct descendant of the nations of the ancient Roman Empire. He will be the head of what will become a new global government which appears will evolve from the European Union.

- The world will welcome the charismatic new leader as he proclaims solutions to the crisis the world is experiencing following the unexplained disappearance of masses of people.

- Due to the weakening of the United States dollar resulting from the massive meltdown of global financial markets and unprecedented debt, many countries are looking for an alternative currency to the dollar and demanding a global currency. The Euro is a possibility, but there are other global currencies being considered.

8

YOU CAN RUN BUT
YOU CAN'T HIDE

*I*n order to successfully take control of the planet the admired world ruler destined to become a brutal dictator will require sophisticated technology that didn't exist until a few years ago. The technology we take for granted today will provide the gateway for this diabolical ruler to dominate the lives of the world's population in the midst of unprecedented devastation tomorrow. Everything this tyrant of the future requires is commercially available now for the first time in history.

THE RACE FOR SPACE

Most, if not all, of the development of new technologies in the last fifty years has been directly or indirectly driven by the research supporting the various space exploration programs. The venture into space was formally initiated when Russia launched the first satellite into orbit on October

4, 1957. The race for space climaxed with the first landing on the moon by the United States on July 20, 1969. However, space exploration continued to advance beyond the first landing on the moon with the American space shuttle program, the Russian manned space program, the launch of the Hubble telescope, the International Space Laboratory program, and various programs to send unmanned space probes to explore Mars and other planets. These programs and associated research have resulted in a phenomenal acceleration of knowledge and commercialization of new technology vital to fulfilling the predictions of the ancient manuscripts.

ELECTRONIC WONDER

My first job after college was as an engineer working for NASA in a department that supported the flight of manned spacecraft. One of my first assignments was to manually check input data for a simulation of computer programs used by the Burroughs computer. This monstrous electronic machine controlled the critical flight paths for the first manned rockets. An army of engineers and technicians was required for operation and maintenance and the state-of-the art machine occupied a room the size of a small house. However, computer technology has advanced like wildfire in the last fifty years. Today almost everything we use is designed, manufactured, driven, bottled, boxed, controlled, tested, checked, operated or eliminated by computers. The development of the microchip even made it possible to manufacture powerful computers smaller than the size of your hand with lightning-fast computing speed. Today you can text people almost anywhere in the world and send pictures almost instantly using an inexpensive cell phone. Modern technology has revolutionized the world of communication and data transmittal and storage.

These advances in electronics and computer development are accelerating at a speed that makes almost any new electronic product obsolete within a year. The integration of this advanced computer expertise with new sophisticated products of modern technology will provide the Antichrist the tools necessary to control the world.

A CASHLESS WORLD SOCIETY

In order for the Antichrist to be successful in his quest to rule the world cash must be totally eliminated from all global financial transactions, regardless of how small or large. Only then can the movement of goods, currency and even people be tracked, located precisely in time and space and recorded for future reference.

Fifty years ago the computer technology, electronics and technical expertise to develop such a global cashless structure didn't exist. There was also no motivation to restructure existing financial systems. However, since the meltdown of worldwide financial markets beginning in 2007, there is a concern about the lack of security, stability and regulation and oversight that permitted the collapse. The leaders of the twenty most industrialized nations in the world (known as the G20) are working to develop the best method to implement a massive overhaul of world financial markets and provide the controls necessary to prevent such an event from occurring again. One of the ideas is to create a common global financial system or a cashless world society since most corporate transactions worldwide are already electronic.

There are other financial undercurrents to encourage nations to support and even expedite a global, cashless financial system. The United States government probably loses billions of tax dollars each year as a result of cash transactions that can't be traced. There are offshore financial transactions made to avoid taxes that are difficult and expensive to investigate by the U.S. government. Therefore, governments will embrace the idea of a cashless world society and possibly pass legislation to that effect sooner rather than later. The world is laying the groundwork for the dictator of the future.

DON'T TAKE THAT NUMBER

During the last half of the invasion, the Antichrist will utilize a sophisticated, cashless, totally electronic global financial system to complete the final step in his diabolical plan to control the world and the people in it. As we know, the only way to gain access to any electronic computer-driven financial system is to have a personal identification number (PIN) and a protected password. Therefore, all the Antichrist has to do is control the PIN in a universal electronic financial system, and he will control the world and everything in it. No one will be able to buy or sell food and goods or make any kind of financial transaction without the acceptance of what is generally referred to as the mark of the Antichrist or what I call the PIN of the Antichrist.[1]

This mark will likely be promoted as a coded personal identification number (PIN) that can't be stolen, duplicated or counterfeited. Of course, each person will have their own protected password. The PIN will also contain all the personal financial information and records of the individual necessary for financial transactions. This PIN will contain an encrypted identifier for the Antichrist and will allow each person with a valid PIN access to the revolutionary global, cashless financial system. However, if you're living during this devastating time, whatever you do, **DON'T** take that number.

One of the technologies the Antichrist requires is a system to quickly, accurately and permanently assign the

PIN to individuals. He will also need to identify, validate, track and monitor the movement of millions, perhaps billions, of people around the world with the PIN, as well as locate those individuals without it. For many years the only method available to make a permanent mark on individuals for identification was a visible ink tattoo, similar to the one used by the Nazis to identify the Jews. However, a conventional tattoo does not provide a means to store the information required to effectively execute financial transactions and there is no easy way to validate the presence of the tattoo on a mass basis. There will have to be a faster, more reliable technology to implement the PIN system, store and retrieve information and validate the presence of the PIN on individuals. A technology is commercially available today in most countries that can accomplish all these tasks and you probably used it several times today.

IT STARTED IN THE GROCERY STORE

In September 1969, members of the Grocery Manufacturers of America (GMA) met with their counterparts of the National Association of Food Chains (NAFC) to discuss an 'inter-industry product code.' Professionals of both groups had independently reached the conclusion that productivity could be improved if a standard method of identifying products were developed. Although everyone agreed that a standard product code was both feasible and desirable, they could not agree on the number of digits in the code. However, the idea was born that eventually resulted in what we know today as the Universal Product Code or bar code identification system exemplified by the symbol similar to the example in the illustration.[2]

Example of UPC Bar Code
Drawing by J.E. Bouvier

It's probably been years since you've seen the actual prices of items displayed on the products you purchase. There is a good likelihood that the labels today have only a series of black vertical bars of different widths separated by white spaces seen in the illustration. This system of bars and spaces is commonly called a bar code or the Universal Product Code (UPC) Bar Code in the United States. These bar codes "talk" to a laser scanner in the hands of the salesperson and have a wealth of information stored on them including the price of the product, the store where it was purchased and the manufacturer. The scanner sends the information to a computer, registers your purchase, and tells the salesperson how much change to give you all in the blink of an eye. A salesperson's involvement in the transaction is obviously minimal.

Today, the bar code system is a mature commercial technology used around the world. "A European numbering system EAN, based on the same principles as the U.P.C., was set in motion in 1974 and has grown rapidly. Over eighty countries now have organizations similar to the Uniform Code Council that issues numbers compatible with the U.P.C."[3] Bar coding is a technology that the Antichrist could easily implement to affix the mark on those accepting his plan. This mark may be in the form of a bar code tattoo. With little difficulty, he will also be able to arrange the location of laser scanners similar to those used in department stores to check individuals for the presence of his mark prior to authorizing a financial transaction. The laser, which is a part of daily life today and a tool the Antichrist will need, was demonstrated for the first time in 1960.

Hospitals today use bar coded bracelets to ensure the identity of patients and newborn babies and to validate their medications and procedures. A recent bank commercial on television humorously illustrated a person waiting in line to make a transaction with a bar code stenciled on his forehead. The teller "swiped" his head across a scanner on the counter to download all the information necessary to complete his transaction. The producers of that commercial probably don't realize how close they are to making a commercial for the Antichrist.

The down side to this technology is that the bar code on an object or person must be in close proximity to a scanner to obtain a valid reading. This means that validating the codes from thousands of people will be cumbersome and extremely time-consuming. However, there is an even more fascinating technology available today that will resolve the logistics problems associated with the bar code system. You probably also used this technology today.

COMPLETELY PAINLESS

There is a technology now commercially available that provides all the advantages of bar coding but is faster and more practical. This electronically-driven technology is called an RFID or Radio Frequency Identification Device. This device uses a "tag" or label that is usually glued on or incorporated inside a product for the purpose of identification. If you have ever used an employee identification badge to enter the office building where you work or if you have used a toll road permit on your automobile (EZ Tag in Houston, Texas), then you have used an RFID. In fact, if you have a late model vehicle you may have noticed that the ignition key looks different from a conventional key. That's because the key contains an RFID that communicates with the anti-theft deterrent system in the automobile and allows you to start the car.

Unlike the barcode which must be indelibly stenciled or tattooed on the surface of the skin the RFID technology has been miniaturized to the point that a small electronic "chip" containing all your personal information can be painlessly implanted under the skin to permanently identify the individual.[4]

In October 2004 the FDA approved the implantation of RFID chips manufactured by Verichip Corp. in humans. "The Food and Drug Administration said Wednesday that Applied Digital Solutions of Delray Beach, Fla., could market the VeriChip, an implantable computer chip about the size of a grain of rice, for medical purposes. With the pinch of a syringe, the microchip is inserted under the skin in a procedure that takes less than 20 minutes and leaves no stitches. Silently and invisibly, the dormant chip stores a code that releases patient specific information when a scanner is passed over it."[5]

With advances in technology, the microchips are becoming even smaller. Soon they may be almost microscopic making the implant process completely painless. "The microchips have already been implanted in 1 million pets. But the chip's possible dual use for tracking people's movements-as well as speeding delivery of their medical information to emergency rooms-has raised alarm. To kick start the chip's use among humans, Applied Digital will provide $650 scanners for free at 200 of the nations trauma centers. The company's chief executive officer, Scott R. Silverman, is one of a dozen executives who had chips implanted. Silverman said chips implanted for medical uses could also be used for security purposes, like tracking employee's movement through nuclear power plants."[6]

In the Texas toll road system an electronic pad ("tag") with an RFID installed is placed on the windshield of vehicles to permit subscribers to pass through the toll booths and have the toll automatically deducted from the subscriber's bank account without stopping the vehicle. EZ Tag has proven that the RFID may be a better technology to quickly and efficiently read the encrypted code in humans at a significant distance without having the person stop in front of a scanner. The toll booth scanners located ten to twenty feet above the highway read the EZ Tags on vehicles as they speed through the toll gates at sixty miles per hour or faster. It will be relatively easy to track the movement of people and check for the presence of the PIN with this technology. You can run, but you can't hide.

I'M WATCHING YOU

There have also been incredible developments in technology that add reality to other events that will take place during the invasion of earth. For example, we'll see later that two mysterious visitors from another dimension will suddenly appear on earth in the Middle East after the evacuation of the "Chosen." When their mission on earth is complete, these men will be murdered by the Antichrist right in the streets of Jerusalem and the entire world will watch them die. Until the commercialization of television, computers, satellites and the complex infrastructure that supports them, there was no way for the entire world to watch any event simultaneously as it is taking place. Today the world can view almost any event while it's actually happening almost anywhere in the world or even in outer space.

In 1969, millions of people watched Neil Armstrong on live television take his first step on the moon more than 200,000 miles from earth. In May of 2008 people all over the world watched the robotic spacecraft Phoenix broadcast pictures of the planet Mars by live television more than 420 million miles away. Closer to home, anyone with internet access can "Google" images taken from satellites in orbit high above the earth. People are able to view clear pictures of their homes and even their cars in the driveways. Remember, this is a technology available to everyone. Think of the power of the satellite imaging technology kept secret and reserved for use by the government for military and national security reasons.

Finally, we know the Antichrist will have no trouble tracking and locating those who become a threat to his diabolical schemes. A satellite-driven technology called a global positioning system, or GPS, is available on many of the cars and trucks today. This technology allows someone to see the exact location of your vehicle at any given moment. In addition, that person can monitor the operation of the engine in your vehicle, check the pressure in your tires or even open a locked door with a push of a button. New cell phones are also likely equipped with GPS.

A person with the implantable microchip technology just discussed will essentially be carrying a personal GPS in his body that can be tracked anywhere. The methods the Antichrist will have to monitor the movement of the population of the world and control their ability to survive was thought to be impossible just a few years ago. Today it's a stark reality. With all the technology available, a person should not be at all surprised to hear someone say, "I'm watching you," because it is probably true.

REFLECTION

- The commercialization of sophisticated technologies that must come to pass before the Antichrist can successfully take control of the planet is here today. The world is ready for the Antichrist.

9

ARE WE THERE YET?

$\mathcal{J}$f you have small children or grandchildren, you are no stranger to the chant, "Are we there yet?" coming from the backseat of your vehicle every few minutes as soon as you leave the driveway to begin a road trip. Children quickly get impatient and want to know when they will arrive at their destination. By now you may be impatient and wondering how close do the "signs" say we are to the beginning of the end of the world? How much time do we have until the end?

Learn how the signs we've already passed on life's highway and those just ahead in our path firmly establish our relative location to Armageddon. They all seem to be pointing to the generation targeted for destruction. Are we there yet? No, but you will be shocked to see how dangerously close we are!

SIGNS WE HAVE ALREADY PASSED

A NEW NATION

The first significant sign of the "beginning of the end" was fulfilled almost 2,000 years after the "Doomsday Clock" abruptly stopped. The Roman Empire destroyed the city of Jerusalem and expelled the Jews from Israel in A.D. 70. The Jews lost their identity as a nation and were scattered across the known world. For nearly two thousand years they lived as citizens in almost every nation in the world; however, they always retained their identity as Jews. Approximately 2,600 years ago, a prediction was documented in the ancient manuscripts that one day the Jews would come from all parts of the world and become the nation of Israel again in what was once their own land.[1] Since history had never recorded the re-emergence of a nation that had been destroyed and its people dispersed, fulfillment of this prediction seemed unlikely, if not impossible, for the Jewish people.

However, the beginning of the return of the Jews to their homeland was the signing of the Balfour declaration in 1917 and the remarkable story of how a Jew was used as the catalyst to bring about this amazing event. "World War I wasn't going well for England. The United Kingdom was desperate to find a method of manufacturing TNT quickly in order to repel the advancement of the Germans (and nothing makes a 'noise' quite like TNT). A brilliant Jew named Chaim Weizmann invented a formula that made rapid production possible, which helped to change the course of the war. In return, the prime minister of England told Dr. Weizmann to name his reward. Rejecting personal recompense, Weizmann requested that Palestine be declared the national homeland for the Jewish people. As a result, the Balfour Declaration was subsequently drafted and signed on November 2, 1917."[2] Approximately thirty one years later, in

1948, Israel was officially recognized as an independent state by the United Nations. The establishment of the homeland of the Jews precisely fulfilled a 2,600-year-old prediction against all odds and marked the first major sign of the beginning of the end. After this world shaking event, the pace of fulfilled signs on the road to Armageddon began to accelerate and suddenly the world was on an unavoidable collision course with destiny.

THE PHOENIX HAS TAKEN FLIGHT

Ancient manuscripts recorded by Daniel describe a world government made up of a federation of nations that must emerge from the ashes of the ancient Roman Empire like the mythical bird Phoenix. This global government will provide the political springboard for the Antichrist to assume control of the world during the invasion of earth. The current federation of European nations appropriately called the European Union that has its roots in the nations of the ancient Roman Empire, is in place today and appears to fulfill that prophecy. Although the metamorphosis of the new world government is not complete, the long-awaited Phoenix has taken flight!

HIS DAY HAS COME

The incredible technology necessary for the fulfillment of events predicted to occur during the invasion of earth is commercially available today. The shrewd master of deception that we call the Antichrist has been waiting patiently in the shadows of time for those technologies to be conceived and developed. He doesn't have to wait any longer for the tools he will need to take over the world. His day has arrived!

WARS, FAMINE, DISEASE AND EARTHQUAKES

Signs that the ancient manuscripts promise will usher in the coming invasion include an unbelievable increase in wars, famine, disease and earthquakes throughout the world.[3]

A TICKING TIME BOMB

Man has been engaged in warfare as long as there was something to be gained by fighting. In just the last 100 years the world has seen WW I, WW II, the war in Vietnam, the Gulf War, the Korean War, the war in Iraq, and now the war in Afghanistan. There are hundreds of wars, battles and revolutions going on today in many small countries and provinces around the world. Terrorists' attacks are escalating at an alarming rate. There is even mounting evidence that nuclear war may soon be a reality. The number of countries brandishing recently developed nuclear warhead capability is increasing at a shocking rate. Iran is known to be developing weapons-grade radioactive material under the cloak of nuclear power for peaceful uses; some people believe they will have a nuclear bomb by 2011. They began testing the operation of their first nuclear powered electrical generating plant in August 2010 heightening fears that they are close to having access to a source of radioactive material which could be used in weapons of mass destruction. Iran also successfully launched a missile capable of deploying a nuclear warhead to neighboring Israel.

In 2003 North Korea withdrew from the 1968 nuclear non-proliferation arms treaty and reactivated a nuclear power plant. In April 2009, North Korea drew fire from NATO, as well as the United States and other countries, for successfully launching a missile believed to be capable of deploying a nuclear warhead to the shores of Alaska. News agencies around the world reported in May 2009, that

North Korea had successfully tested a nuclear bomb that some sources estimate was about the same strength as the bomb dropped on Hiroshima, Japan. In May 2010, North Korea threatened war against South Korea if they retaliated for the alleged torpedoing of one of their ships. Pakistan and India also have nuclear warhead capability although neither were signatory to the 1968 nuclear non-proliferation arms treaty. The world is a ticking time bomb!

A POPULATION EXPLOSION

There continues to be an increase in the number of people worldwide starving to death and suffering from disease. The world is bulging from a population that has exploded to more than six billion people in the last fifty years. Thousands die daily of malnutrition and disease in spite of well-meaning charity programs that provide massive airlifts with food and fresh water. Many in the United States are stockpiling food and water and other supplies in anticipation of severe shortages and potential famine.

Thousands of people have died in recent years due to outbreaks of pandemic flu throughout the world including the "Asian flu" in the 1950's and the "Hong Kong flu" in the 1960's. The pandemic bird flu in Asia caused worldwide panic in 2005. The United States declared a public health emergency in 2009 due to the outbreak and spread of the infectious swine flu that originated in Mexico. In September 2009, cases of H1N1 (swine flu) were reported in all fifty states in the United States and many parts of the world. The congested working conditions in large cities and travel in crowded modes of modern international transportation quickly spread any pandemic disease. AIDS also continues to be a major health issue in the world in spite of the millions of dollars expended annually to control it. The world is surrendering lives every minute to disease and famine.

THE FURY OF PLANET EARTH

Planet earth is also doing its part to fulfill ancient prophecies. Although new technology makes it easier to identify and catalog the occurrence and frequency of earthquakes, massive storms and volcanic eruptions around the world every year, it seems they are now more prevalent in number and intensity than ever.

In 2004, one of the largest recorded earthquakes in history occurred in the Indian Ocean generating a tsunami that was responsible for the deaths of more than 200,000 people. In 2005, Hurricane Katrina slammed into the United States Gulf Coast causing massive damage in Louisiana and Mississippi. This storm all but wiped out the city of New Orleans. A massive earthquake struck Pakistan in 2005 killing approximately 75,000 people and injuring more than 100,000. In May 2008, a cyclone hit Burma that reportedly caused as many as 100,000 deaths. In September 2008, hurricane Ike, the size of the state of Texas, hit the Texas Gulf Coast and devastated the island of Galveston, causing widespread damage.

In January 2010, a mammoth 7.0 earthquake struck Haiti reportedly killing more than 100,000 people and affecting the lives of more than 3,000,000 others. A deadly 8.8 earthquake struck Chile in March 2010 sending tsunamis across the Pacific Ocean with a second earthquake hitting Argentina a few hours later. Recently, regions around the world have been rattled by earthquakes striking areas that have never felt the ground shake. In April 2010, the world was given a preview of the havoc that can be triggered by the eruption of a single strategically-located volcano. Eyjafiallajokull, a volcano beneath a glacier in southern Iceland that had been dormant since 1983, suddenly made its presence known to the world again. In a magnificent declaration of fury the infamous crater spewed clouds of blinding ash several miles into the skies blanketing much of northern Europe with erosive debris. In addition to the local damage and deaths in Iceland, the veil of ash totally paralyzed air traffic in Europe and other parts of the world for days.

If earthquakes, tsunamis, cyclones, hurricanes and volcanoes aren't enough to test mankind, we are now seeing the effects of global warming. It's debatable whether this phenomenon is a result of the abuse of the earth by mankind or a natural cycle. However, it's reported that the ice caps have been shrinking at a disturbing rate in the last fifty years. Glaciers centuries old are retreating, leaving deep gouges and creating new lakes in the earth where none previously existed. Global weather patterns are changing, and the ocean levels are predicted to rise. It's as though the bowels of the planet are groaning with pain under the ever increasing weight of mankind's selfish abuse of the planet. However, once the invasion commences, the earth will be free to execute deadly supernatural strikes of nature against her tenants that will be absolutely unimaginable.

SIGNS JUST AHEAD

EVACUATION OF THE "CHOSEN"

One fact we know for sure is that the invasion will not begin until the "Chosen" has been safely evacuated from earth to safety. As of the writing of this book that hasn't happened, but it could occur at any moment!

THE LAST JIHAD

More than 2,600 years ago a prophecy was recorded in the ancient manuscripts that described a military invasion of the modern nation of Israel by a coalition of primarily Muslim nations.[4] With the daily news alive with the never-ending turmoil in the Middle East, it's not difficult to imagine the prophecy of such a coalition of nations attempting to eradicate the nation of Israel in a massive "hate" invasion. However, in Muslim terminology, this will be "the last jihad." With the escalation of conflict in the Middle East, terrorist attacks worldwide, and threats of nuclear war since the 9/11 attack on the United States the world is teetering on the fault line of the last jihad which could take place any day.

The ancient manuscripts describe "… an invasion of the land of Israel in the last days by a vast confederation of nations from north of the Black and Caspian Seas, extending down to modern Iran in the east, as far as modern Libya to the west, and down to Sudan in the south. Therefore, Russia will have at least five key allies: Turkey, Iran, Libya, Sudan, and the Islamic nations of the former Soviet Union. Amazingly, all of these nations are Muslim nations, and Iran, Libya and Sudan are three of Israel's most ardent opponents."[5]

Iran seems to be on everyone's list of nations that make up the coalition. Iranian President Mahmoud Ahmadinejad, was elected to office in 2005 and re-elected in 2009. He wasted no time expressing his desire to aggressively destroy Israel and the United States. "Upon taking office, Ahmadinejad took a series of moves that sent shock waves through world capitals, rattled global markets, and drove up the international price of oil. He told associates that he believed the end of the world was just two or three years away. He said he believed he had been chosen by Allah to become Iran's leader at this critical hour to hasten the coming of the Islamic messiah known as the Twelfth Imam or the Mahdi by launching a final holy war against Christians and Jews. He publicly vowed to annihilate the

United States. He vowed to wipe Israel 'off the map.'"[6] It is now common knowledge that Iran is very close to having a nuclear bomb and a launch vehicle capable of delivering the weapon of mass destruction to Israel. It will only be a matter of time before Iran has missiles capable of reaching more distant targets. "Americans are deeply divided over whether the U.S. should take pre-emptive military action against Iran. What's more, even if the American president was to do so, Iranian leaders say 'any invader will find Iran to be a burning Hell for them.' If attacked, Iran has vowed to retaliate by unleashing a wave of 40,000 suicide bombers against American, Israeli, and European targets and into Iraq. The plan, which includes activating some fifty terrorist sleeper cells allegedly pre-positioned in the U.S., Canada, and Europe to use chemical and biological warfare against civilian and industrial targets, is ominously code-named Judgment Day."[7]

President Ahmadinejad was invited to speak at the United Nations in September 2008. He "… addressed the U.N. General Assembly Tuesday declaring that the 'American empire' is nearing collapse and should end its military involvement in other countries. Ahmadinejad also lashed out at Israel on Tuesday, saying the Zionist regime is on a definite slope to collapse, and there is no way for it to get out of the cesspool created by itself and its supporters… The Iranian president is feared and reviled in Israel because of his repeated calls to wipe the Jewish state off the map, and his aggressive pursuit of nuclear technology has only fueled Israel's fears… 'A few bullying powers have sought to put hurdles in the way of the peaceful nuclear activities of the Iranian nation by exerting political and economic pressures against Iran,' he said."[8] Did that sound like a threat? In 2010 President Ahmadinejad again spoke at the United Nations and promised to continue with their nuclear program for "peaceful purposes."

Of course, the timing of an attack on Israel by the Muslim coalition will likely be accelerated if Israel's strongest and perhaps only ally, the United States, steps aside from the threat of conflict. In 1973, a coalition of Arab nations led by Egypt and Syria and backed by the military support of the Soviet Union aggressively attacked Israel. When the Soviets threatened to attack Israel directly, President Nixon and the United States made it clear they were committed to the support of Israel and would not back down from aggression. Following a heightened military presence of U.S. forces in the Middle East tensions were defused, a nuclear war between the two super powers was averted and a cease-fire was achieved. Will the United States provide the same kind of unyielding unilateral support to Israel in the event of a threatened attack by the Muslim coalition?

The Muslim nations will attack Israel like a storm and cover the land like a blanket but Israel will not be defeated. There is an incredible description of the predicted defeat of the Muslim coalition in the ancient manuscripts. A massive earthquake will disrupt the attack on Israel and will be felt by the entire world. It's likely that the quake will disrupt communications, destroy land forces and confuse those responsible for developing strategy and deploying military forces. In addition, a deadly disease or virus, perhaps a pandemic flu, is predicted to infest the armies of the coalition rendering the personnel ill and ineffective for battle. Hailstone and fire will rain down on the enemy destroying men and equipment.[9]

Imagine other mysterious events that may take place during this foiled assault that are not mentioned in the ancient manuscripts. Ground-to-air missiles aimed at Israel will be destroyed on their launching pads and invading aircraft from the coalition will never reach the border of Israel. On the way to their targets they will mysteriously disappear from radar destroyed by the rain of hail and fire. Israel will scramble their interceptor jets only to find the skies strangely vacant of the enemy. Finally, the manuscripts indicate that the "weapon of confusion" will be used against the Muslim coalition to create the greatest number of "friendly fire" casualties ever encountered in warfare. There will be such a large number of the enemy killed that it will take the Israelites seven months just to bury the dead.[10] The birds and beasts of the land will be invited to eat the flesh and drink the blood of the bodies. The last jihad will be stopped dead in its tracks. The invading military forces will be reduced to mountains of corpses and their strategic war machines will be converted to massive piles of useless scrap.

The fact that it will take the Israelites seven years to destroy and burn the weapons of war as predicted in the ancient manuscripts gives us a definite clue to the timing of this ill-fated Muslim assault on Israel.[11] The Israelites will be forced to go into hiding for the last three-and-one-half years of the invasion to escape an attack by the Antichrist. If they are in hiding, they cannot be burning the weapons of war belonging to the Muslim coalition of nations. The destruction of the weapons must be complete before the mid-point of the invasion. Therefore, simple math would conclude that this war should take place approximately seven years before the Israelites flee Israel or three-and-one-half years before the invasion begins.

SIGN THE TREATY

The Antichrist will be firmly entrenched in his position of power in the European Union infrastructure and will have garnered the support of world leaders by the time the Muslim coalition of nations attack Israel. In addition, the popular politician boasting a policy of peaceful diplomacy will likely court the nation of Israel as a committed ally and may even take credit for secretly sabotaging the Muslim coalition in their attempted invasion of Israel resulting in their overwhelming defeat. This presumed demonstration of allegiance to Israel will be the gateway to entertaining their leaders with his desire to make a covenant or agreement for seven years of peace and security.[12] "Antichrist, on behalf of his empire, will make a treaty with the nation of Israel. This agreement probably entails a promise of protection in return for certain favors (likely including those of an economic nature). It is easy to understand why Israel would enter into such an agreement with the powerful forces of Antichrist. With such protection Israel will feel safe and secure from a world of intruders. The term of the treaty will be promised 'for one seven,' that is seven years."[13]

When the Antichrist signs the treaty with Israel the "Doomsday Clock" will be activated again and begin to count down seven agonizing years of suffering, pain and anguish for mankind. However, the Antichrist does not intend to keep his agreement with Israel or the rest of the world. He will break the covenant with Israel halfway through the invasion, a period of three-and-one-half years after it begins.

The next two events may begin before or even during the early years of the seven-year invasion.

ONE GLOBAL FINANCIAL SYSTEM

A worldwide "cashless" electronic system that the Antichrist will require to control goods, services and people is already in the planning stages by some of the largest industrialized nations to avoid a future global meltdown of financial markets and may soon be just one transaction away.

THE THIRD TEMPLE

For more than a thousand years the Temple in Jerusalem in ancient Israel had a special place in the spiritual lives of the Israelites. The Temple was the centerpiece for the worship of the God of the Israelites, and the Holy of Holies in the Temple was the anointed place for the sacrificial offerings. However, the first permanent Temple in Jerusalem was destroyed in 586 B.C. by Nebuchadnezzar, King of Babylon an arch enemy of the Israelites.

Construction on a second Temple was started in 538 B.C. by King Zerubbabel, of Judah, but the Temple was later desecrated and plundered by King Antiochus IV, of Syria. In approximately 20 B.C., King Herod rebuilt and enlarged the second Temple, which was in a great state of disrepair. However, in A.D. 70 the second Temple was destroyed by the Romans and exists today only in ruins on the Temple Mount in Jerusalem.

Although there is no Jewish Temple in Jerusalem today, the manuscripts predict that about the mid-point of the invasion, the Antichrist will go to the "Holy of Holies" in the Jewish Temple where the sacrifices are made. He will desecrate or defile this sacred place by declaring him to be a god.[14] The Antichrist's actions will so pollute the Temple that the Jewish people will no longer permit it to be used for ceremonial practices, and the Temple will be desolate and empty. This act will be an absolute atrocity to the Jewish people and is commonly referred to as an abomination of desolation. "One who causes desolation refers to the Antichrist, who will forbid worship and thereby make the Temple area desolate (empty). Rather than being an object that desolates in this context, it appears to be the Antichrist himself who desolates".[15] Since there is no Jewish Temple today, a third or new Temple must be constructed in Jerusalem and be operational before the mid-point of the invasion. "The restoration of the earthly Temple… apparently will take place prior to the mid-point of the seventieth week, since at that point the 'abomination of desolation' will have taken place in its Holy Place."[16]

At the present time, the most famous Islamic shrine in Jerusalem, the Dome of the Rock, is sitting directly on top of what is believed to be the location of the ruins of the ancient Temple of Jerusalem preventing construction of a new Temple. Granted, it may take an "act of God" to construct a new Temple without starting another war in the Middle East, but this Temple must be rebuilt. It's interesting that there have been several earthquakes in the vicinity of the Dome of the Rock in the last ten years. In fact, in 2008 an earthquake created a large hole in the Temple Mount Plaza just a short distance from the Dome itself. Perhaps a natural disaster will eliminate the Dome of the rock and prepare the foundation for the new Temple.

"Many plans are being made for a rebuilt Temple and many diverse groups in Israel are preparing for it."[17] A group called the Temple Institute, led by Israel Ariel "…has made almost all the 102 utensils needed for Temple worship according to biblical and rabbinic standards. These are on display for tourists to see at the Temple Institute tourist center in the Old City of Jerusalem."[18] The plan is coming together.

THE "TERMINAL GENERATION"

Daniel was instructed by the strange messenger to preserve the manuscripts documenting the information he was given about the future because it will be critically relevant for the generation targeted by the invasion of earth. That generation alone will recognize the fulfillment of signs indicating the end of the world is near and will search the manuscripts to understand more about the coming invasion.[19]

The fig tree has historically been representative of Israel. Most scholars agree that the reference to the "fig tree sprouting leaves" recorded in the ancient manuscripts is the prophecy of the reinstatement of the nation of Israel that occurred in 1948.[20] Since this prophecy is also believed to reference the "end times," we may conclude that the generation which saw the state of Israel recognized as a nation in 1948 may be the targeted generation. Many of those born in 1948 are young enough to live another twenty or even thirty years. It's becoming clear that the evacuation of the "Chosen" may be as close as tomorrow's sunrise!

REFLECTIONS

Before we explore the shocking, graphic details of the invasion of earth, let's reflect on what we have learned in the last few chapters about the major events and signs that establish how close the world is to the invasion of earth and Armageddon.

The following have already come to pass:

- All the technology required for the Antichrist to take control of the world is commercially available today.

- The formation of a coalition of nations out of the ashes of the Roman Empire will provide the political springboard for the Antichrist to rule the world as described by Daniel more than 2,600 years ago. It appears that the new government has arrived embodied in the European Union which is continuing to evolve towards complete fulfillment of the ancient prophecy.

- The establishment of the nation of Israel in1948 fulfilled an ancient prophecy that for centuries seemed absolutely impossible.

- The emergence of a new foreign policy of peaceful diplomacy rather than the use of military strength to avoid conflict has been adopted by the European Union and embraced by the Barack Obama White House administration of the United States.

- The Euro was established as the currency for the European Union and is quickly gaining international acceptance as a new world currency while the American dollar continues to lose value and respect in international markets. Many countries are demanding a new global currency.

- We appear to be experiencing a dramatic increase in wars, famine, disease and natural disasters throughout the world.

- The Middle East continues to boil with the mounting aggression of Muslim nations towards Israel and her allies.

- The financial meltdown of global capital markets has prompted plans to make sweeping changes in the infrastructure of global financial markets.

The following signs are just ahead

- **THE EVACUATION OF THE "CHOSEN" FROM EARTH TO SAFETY.**

- The invasion of Israel by a Muslim coalition.

- The negotiation of a seven-year peace treaty by the Antichrist with Israel for protection, which <u>will actually activate the "Doomsday Clock" and initiate the invasion.</u>

- The building of the third Temple in Jerusalem.

- The implementation of a global, cashless financial system.

10

THE CLOCK IS
TICKING-AGAIN

*B*y now you have a very clear image of the man who will rule the world during the invasion of earth as well as the government that will ultimately provide a diplomatic springboard for his entry into world politics. This popular politician will arrive on the European scene boasting of his passion to heal the planet crippled by the unexplained disappearance of hundreds of millions of people. However, this self-proclaimed physician for the world's ailments will harbor a secret, diabolical agenda for those remaining on earth. It's astounding to realize the world's leaders will totally embrace this relatively unknown, charismatic politician who will emerge from the shadows with limited evidence of his political experience, vague background and training. It's even more amazing that they will propel him to a pedestal of unbelievable power that he will use to take possession of the world with their overwhelming approval and encouragement. Although the ancient manuscripts are silent as to how the Antichrist will actually make his debut in the world of politics and rise to power, imagine the following very plausible scenario.

RISE TO POWER

After the "Chosen" is evacuated from earth to safety, the planet will fall helplessly into a state of uncontrolled pandemonium, due to the impact of the unexplained disappearance of so many people from the world. In fact, every single person who is removed to safety will impact, in some way, the lives of those who are left. Tragically, many family units will be fractured as some are taken and others are left, confused and panic-stricken. The world will experience a global crisis significantly worse than the meltdown of the financial markets beginning in 2007. The civil unrest and riots in Greece in 2010 caused by the austere government policies enacted to save the nation from bankruptcy provide a relevant preview of what will be encountered worldwide. The global disorder and uncontrolled panic will serve as the perfect catalyst for the history-making introduction of the Antichrist to the world.

The man destined to rule the world will arrive on the scene quietly, supported by a robust network of powerful influential supporters who are politically connected. These advocates will be organized by a very influential man we will call the Minister of Propaganda described by John as a demon in a lamb's suit or false prophet.[1] He's an imposter, a political "spin doctor" who will precede the Antichrist masquerading as an astute, experienced, mild-mannered public relations man well-respected by the media. By achieving a powerful position in the government and garnering support and respect from top officials, the Minister of Propaganda will pave the way for the Antichrist. In this role he will be the spokesman for the Antichrist in all matters, the only outlet for information to the general population. Any media personnel who choose not to be supportive of the Antichrist will be quietly silenced. With his charismatic, articulate speaking ability and demonic demeanor, this slick Minister of Propaganda will easily persuade the liberal media and powerful political supporters to launch the record-breaking career of the Antichrist. They will provide the diplomatic rocket that puts him on a trajectory to attaining positions of increasing authority, responsibility and control, unparalleled by anyone before him.

World leaders inside and outside the European Union (EU) will quickly recognize the Antichrist as an individual who has outstanding potential in matters of global finance, fiscal and monetary economic policy, diplomatic relations and foreign affairs. His magnetic personality and rock star popularity will immediately capture the hearts of people of all ages and walks of life worldwide. People will be mesmerized by every word when he speaks, and the liberal media will often afford him that opportunity. In addition, the Antichrist's proven ability to embrace the soft political diplomacy of the EU will win him immediate support for appointment to a prominent position in foreign policy. His nomination for the Nobel Peace prize will be a worthy tribute to his development of revolutionary foreign policies as he forges the new frontier of world peace and diplomacy. With each act of fashionable diplomatic policy, the popularity of the Antichrist will soar to new heights. Many will marvel at how quickly this man has risen to power from the shadows and conclude this charismatic new leader must be the messiah sent to save the world.

As the popularity of the Antichrist continues to rise, he will solicit the support of the scientific community to convince the world that the recent unexplained disappearance of people was due to alien invaders from another galaxy. He will fabricate a monstrous lie that the world will accept without hesitation. With the overwhelming approval of world leaders he will designate a special group of scientists and military personnel to study what can be done to prevent future attacks by the strange invaders. This shrewd, rising star will offer a plan that promises to stabilize the economy, restore order and initiate the repair of damaged infrastructures of nations throughout the world. However, he will explain that his plan requires a fundamental change in the structure of governments worldwide. In order for the rehabilitation of the planet to be efficient, fast and well-organized, a single, or one world, government must be formed on an emergency basis with strict rules and regulations. This new government must also be presided over by an outstanding individual with the ability to effectively lead the world out of turmoil to recovery, someone who is not afraid of making difficult decisions in unchartered territory.

After exhaustive meetings evaluating the proposal of this brilliant new politician, the heads of states of the G20 agree that the only way to quickly rebuild the damaged infrastructure of the world and restore order in the midst of increasing chaos is with a form of unified world government. The new government must be well-coordinated, directed from a single political position and have the power to make decisions free from frequent infighting and bipartisan politics. Finally, the new government must be implemented without delay. World leaders realize the proven structure of the European Union will provide the perfect political model for the new world government. In fact, it will be a straightforward task to simply enlarge the existing organizations and infrastructure of the European Union to accommodate additional member nations of the industrialized world.

Thus, what we will call the New World Order will be born with the overwhelming approval and solid support of the world's leaders. A person must be elected to preside over the new world government. What better candidate for president of the New World Order than the admired, charismatic, captivating politician who is the architect of the new global government? The world leaders will willingly give this widely acclaimed politician control of their nations.[2] They will truly believe he will do the best job of reassuring the population and restoring order. At this point, the new world government will be organized with ten kings, the code word for leaders (with the correct Roman Empire heritage) of nations or regions of the world who will report directly to the Antichrist. The smaller nations, countries and provinces would be divided among the heads of state of the ten larger industrialized nations to form ten global regions and incorporate them into the government of the New World Order. The fulfillment of this final stage of prophecy regarding the new global government of the Antichrist will be natural and easy to implement. A part of the restructuring of the world governments may even support expediting the implementation of a global financial structure growing out of recommendations following the meltdown of financial markets that began in 2007.

Now, the scene momentarily shifts back to the island of Patmos as John waited to hear the next set of instructions from the supernatural messenger. His journey to the future and our breathtaking trip to the end of the world is about to begin.

THE IDENTITY OF THE "INSIDER"

After completing the brief letters to the seven first century congregations of the "Chosen" as instructed, John heard a voice from above that thundered like the sound of a trumpet. The voice resonated in the quietness of the day demanding

John to leave the island and proceed to a location far above the earth.[3] Of course, John had no idea where he was going or the nature of his assignment. Suddenly without warning and before he could even answer, John was supernaturally drawn up through the heavens to a mysterious location. He noticed his mortal body was temporarily transformed to a spiritual state to make the trip.

John soon realized he had been spirited while still alive to that serene, eternal paradise called heaven, a place most people hope is within their grasp after they experience physical death. In the midst of this place of ecstasy, John saw many strange sights, including an awesome being sitting on a throne out of which preceded bolts of lightning and thunder. John knew he was in the very presence of the all-powerful, all-knowing, almighty Creator of the universe and everything that's in it. He was standing in the presence of the mysterious messenger, the "Insider." God revealed His identity in the manuscripts John recorded so there would be no question as to the source and credibility of this relevant insight into the future. The God of the universe then proceeded to supernaturally and realistically bring each of the events of the seven year invasion of earth into view for John to experience as though they were projected onto a life-size three-dimensional screen of the earth. John was about to witness mankind's journey to the end of the world.

God wasn't just going to dictate the chronicle of the future to John. He was going to allow him to personally experience the full impact of the invasion complete with lights, sound and action. From his vantage point, John would see everything as it unfolds throughout the world as if it was actually happening at that time. John could then record what he saw and heard in his own words for the benefit of the future generation targeted by the invasion.

Through the eyes of John we have a box seat view of the invasion before it actually happens.

You will now experience all the shocking, unforgettable details of the incredible insider information narrated by the man who personally witnessed the future from the past and recorded the events for future generations.

THE CODE BOOK

John's attention was drawn to the book that God was holding sealed with seven seals so that it couldn't be opened until this dramatic moment.[4]The code book actually contains the precise sequence of events, detailed instructions and the responsibilities of those who will activate and launch the weapons of mass destruction to the planet. Now we know who planned and who will orchestrate the most cataclysmic invasion imaginable. The supernatural God of the universe who created the earth and everything that's within it will also destroy it.

However, the identity of the One allowing this supernatural attack will elude most of the world's population. Desperate for answers, the majority of civilizations will readily embrace the deceptive propaganda carefully articulated by the Antichrist and his faithful supporters to explain the global holocaust. The world leader will submit that the upheaval of the planet, initiated by the recent abduction of hundreds of millions of people, is being caused by an invading advanced civilization from deep space. The population will be warned to brace for the possibility of more attacks by the unknown invaders.

As John's narration begins, the invasion is divided into three major offensives, with each offensive having seven unique weapons of mass destruction launched at target earth. In the first offensive the opening of each of seven

mysterious seals on the code book for the invasion will
trigger action on the planet.

THE FIRST OFFENSIVE

THE INAUGURAL PROCESSION

When the first seal was broken, the pages of the book
were turned and the invasion began, quietly at first. John
saw a rider on a magnificent white horse.[5] The rider is none
other than the Antichrist, the ruler of the modern world,
but what is he doing? As stated earlier, the treaty with
Israel negotiated by the Antichrist will actually initiate the
invasion of earth that begins with the opening of the first
seal. However, the Antichrist must be on the scene for some
time before the invasion begins in order to win the hearts
of the world's population, gain entrance into the politics
of world government and successfully negotiate the treaty
with Israel.

Perhaps the opening of the first seal simply sets the
stage for the inaugural processional on earth to celebrate
the Antichrist officially taking office as President of the
New World Order, the one-world government. The world
will hail him as the "anointed one" who will restore order to
the earth and protect the world from the invaders. Throngs
of spectators will crowd the streets of the processional and
cheer as this proud new statesman rides by on his superb
white steed flanked by armed security personnel. The rest of
the world will be captivated by the pomp and circumstance
of the ceremonies as they watch by television. The Antichrist
may even be dressed in a uniform representative of his Roman
heritage carrying articles which symbolize his power. John
said he had a bow but he didn't mention any arrows. He was
familiar with the bow and arrow used by Roman archers in
long range combat and probably wondered what possible use

is a bow without arrows? The answer is the Antichrist will use the weapon of seduction and soft peaceful diplomacy rather than weapons of mass destruction to assume control of the earth. The crown on his head tells us the Antichrist will indeed be successful in his quest to rule the earth during the invasion. What a turning point this day will be for the world and the lives of its inhabitants.

WORLD OF WARS

There may be a lapse in time between the inauguration of the Antichrist and the opening of the second seal. The Antichrist will likely have some time to firmly establish his position of power and promise of peace throughout the world following the negotiation of the treaty with Israel. Then John saw that peace in the world was shattered when the second seal was opened and the constraints placed on mankind to maintain peace in the world were removed.[6] Heads of rogue nations will ignore the dire consequences of a "pre-emptive strike" on an armed aggressor and openly wage war against those they hate. Peaceful nations will be forced to join the conflict. The prospect of war will be raised to a level unparalleled since the beginning of time. This "world of wars," or what may be more appropriately referred to as World War III, will only add to the chaos existing before the invasion started. John noticed the heavens now assumed the appearance of a scroll when it is rolled together. This lethal scene in the skies could only be the heart-stopping mushroom–like clouds characteristic of thermonuclear explosions rising thousands of feet into the heavens and spewing deadly radiation into the atmosphere. Nations recklessly deploying their recently acquired nuclear weapons of mass destruction while battling for control of the Middle East oil reserves and executing deadly terrorist attacks will have the world galvanized with fear.

War will quickly deplete the financial and natural resources of nations, reduce the available food supply and interrupt the source of fuel for cars, mass transportation, electrical generating plants and factories. The proliferation of war will intensify the stress on the world's population. If the United States is forced to engage in war, Americans may for the first time since World War II experience the scarcity of the products to which they are accustomed. Just when the temper of the world's population is heated to the boiling point, the next seal is opened.

RUNAWAY INFLATION

When the third seal was opened, John heard a voice say that it would take a penny to buy a measure of wheat or three measures of barley in the world.[7] John knew from experience that a penny was approximately the wages for a man for a full day's work in the first century in which he lived.[8] Therefore, this period of the invasion will be a time of hyper-inflation in the world due in part to the devastating results of the wars. On the other hand, the collapse of global financial markets and unprecedented debt in the world due to unsustainable spending prior to the invasion will likely cause runaway inflation pushing the prices of necessities upward. Famine will be rampant with shortages of food and the necessities of life. There may be a resurgence of bread-lines for those unable to work or provide their family with sufficient food. Supplementary means of support in the United States like social security and government entitlement programs may be non-existent by this time, financially depleted due to the rising number of participants. The world may even experience the effects of hyper-inflation reminiscent of the most fevered moments in Germany's history in 1923 when a wheelbarrow full of cash would not buy a loaf of bread.

1.5 BILLION DIE

When the fourth seal was opened, the world experienced the death of one fourth of the world's population as a result of wars, disease and hunger from the opening of the first three seals.[9] Approximately 1.5 billion people will die based on a remaining population of 6 billion people after the evacuation of the "Chosen." Even the animals and beasts of the earth will be given the license and supernatural power to overpower and kill innocent people. Those who refused to accept the gift of life will be the targets of the destruction of the first four seals. Spiritual representatives of the "dark side" will be on hand to gleefully drag the large number of dead to the land of everlasting darkness on the other side of the grave.

Can you comprehend the deaths of 1.5 billion people? That's more than four times the population of the entire United States in 2010. Mass graves, rather than individual funerals and gravesites, will be used to bury friends and family members, leaving no emotional closure for the living. Disease caused by dead bodies left in the streets will be overwhelming. The loss of so many people will compound the havoc imposed on the world's infrastructures by the recent unexplained disappearance of hundreds of millions of people. One only has to look at the aftermath of the recent earthquake in Haiti in January 2010 where more than 100,000 people died to imagine the chaos that will be rampant during this time.

REVENGE

The opening of the fifth seal seems to be a departure from the devastation on earth as the scene shifts to heaven. When the fifth seal was opened, John saw millions of people in heaven who died during the early years of the invasion.

Since they had not accepted the gift of life before the "Chosen" was evacuated from earth, they were left to live through the invasion. However, they later accepted the gift during the invasion and died as martyrs because they were a stumbling block to the agenda of the ruthless Antichrist. They cried for revenge but were told they must be patient since more people would die as martyrs during the invasion. They were reassured that justice would be served later.

> *Isn't that interesting! It is so difficult for most of us to be patient in this fast-paced world. At one time, we were impatient if things didn't happen in hours or days. Today, we're irritated if our computer network connection doesn't take place in less than a few seconds. Now we're told that even martyrs in heaven must be patient to have their revenge.*

After the brief intermission, death and suffering returns to the inhabitants of the earth as they are subjected to one shocking deadly attack after another.

THE EARTH WOBBLES

It's a scientific fact that the earth has a slight measurable "wobble" or small motion in the axis of rotation relative to the earth's surface. The "wobble" of the earth can be compared to the shaking of an automobile tire slightly out of balance. This insignificant motion of the planet is not serious and has no effect on our lives. However, there have been attempts to correlate the frequency of earthquakes, volcanic activity and even changes in weather patterns with slight changes in the "wobble" of the earth over time. The most frightening fact is that the ancient manuscripts reveal a terrifying prediction that one day the earth will reel to and fro like a drunkard.[10] This serious out-of-balance condition of the planet may result in drastic changes in weather patterns, play havoc with seasonal climates and induce levels of extreme stress on the tectonic plates of the earth creating massive earthquakes, deadly tsunami ocean waves, lethal volcanic activity, etc. On the other hand, massive earthquakes or volcanic activity may actually excite the "wobble" of the earth, making it worse and thus compound the creation of additional natural disasters. The incredible cataclysmic upheaval of the planet as a result of unbelievable natural disasters may, in part, be a result of the unbelievable prediction of increased scientific "wobble" of the earth recorded in ancient manuscripts more than twenty-six hundred years ago.

When the sixth seal was opened, John witnessed the destruction caused by a great earthquake resulting in mountains and islands being completely relocated.[11] An earthquake is a very frightening occurrence as the ground beneath you begins to tremble and the way to safety is often unknown. I can still personally recall being awakened by a loud groaning noise early one morning in a Los Angeles hotel room in 1969. Pictures were falling off the wall and doors were opening and closing. The groaning noise I heard was the sound of nearby structures moving that were not supposed to move including the building I was in. The earthquake was only one of many felt by the residents of Los Angeles, California over the years. It was a terrifying experience I don't want to repeat. Based on that encounter, it is difficult to fathom what the residents of earth will suffer with the opening of the sixth seal.

Historically, earthquakes have caused cracks to open in the ground and buildings to collapse. However, imagine the

Hawaiian Islands in the Pacific Ocean, Grand Cayman in the Caribbean, which is our family's favorite vacation spot, or the hundreds of beautiful Greek islands in the Mediterranean Sea literally being ripped from their foundations in the oceans. It is conceivable that entire islands will suddenly be torn from their resting places and sink into the depths of the sea. They will descend below the waters' surface dragging their inhabitants and everything for miles around down with them. Mammoth cruise ships packed with passengers at nearby docks will be unable to escape their destiny as they accelerate helplessly down a massive watery vortex produced by the sinking islands and disappear beneath the water forever.

Imagine the Rocky Mountains, Mount St. Helens, the Smoky Mountains, Mount Everest and the magnificent European Alps as they are cracked from their bases and shoved away to a distant location. There is no way to comprehend or visualize this kind of massive destruction of such familiar landscape as it is relocated by an unimaginable source of incredible energy. There will be global devastation due to tidal waves, volcanic eruptions, and changes in global weather patterns as a result of the movements in the earth when these massive changes in the planet's landscape and seascape occur. Scientists will be baffled and the world will be panic-stricken.

While the earth is shaking violently from the mammoth earthquake, the world will suddenly be plunged into darkness. Many dormant volcanoes will surge to life as the mountains crack and pressurized magma gush from the bowels of the earth hurling massive amounts of molten rock, ash and dust into the skies. As a result of the ash blanketing the atmosphere only the reddish colors of light from the sun will strike the moon's surface giving it an eerie blood-red color and causing everything on earth to have a sinister dim red glow in the darkness. The population of the earth will be terrified at what looks like a sure omen of the end of the world. In 1972, my wife and I were privileged to witness the spectacular night launch of the NASA Apollo 17 rocket that stood thirty-six stories tall and carried men to the moon and returned them safely to earth. As the mammoth rocket lifted off from Cape Canaveral, the deafening roar of the rocket engines that produced more than seven million pounds of thrust caused the very ground where we were standing to shake and our clothes to visibly flutter against our bodies. The flames from the exhaust of the engines painted the Florida sky a spine-chilling blood-red color, and we heard voices in the crowd murmur, "It looks like the end of the world."

The ash and dust-laden air of the global invasion due to volcanic activity is likely to encircle the entire globe spreading darkness everywhere. Death will come swiftly without warning from volcanoes throughout the world like the historical Mount Vesuvius. This lethal mountain scarred by multiple eruptions over the centuries is located near Naples, Italy. In A.D. 79, the infamous Mount Vesuvius erupted unleashing its fury on the unsuspecting populations of Pompeii and other nearby small towns located in the shadow of the angry mountain. My wife and I recently toured the amazing ruins of Pompeii and had the opportunity to view museum relics of the fateful eruption on the site of that ancient city. The artifacts depicting the instantaneous deaths of people who were residents of Pompeii made an unforgettable and shocking impact on us. The explanation given to us by those familiar with the bizarre deaths was difficult to comprehend. They gave the following account of the deadly eruptions which may very well give us a spine-tingling glimpse into the future of the horror this sixth seal of terror will initiate.

In August A.D. 79 Mount Vesuvius signaled her intent to destroy and kill by sending a massive mushroom cloud of smoke miles into the sky followed by ash raining down on nearby towns as far away as the Aegean seacoast. However, the local residents were not intimidated by the mountain's promise of destruction since they had experienced her empty threats in the past. In the early morning hours of August 24, A.D. 79, the molten rock from deep in the earth rushed to the surface of Mount Vesuvius in a massive explosion to create one of the infamous volcano's deadliest performances in history. As the molten magma burst from the throat of the volcano, the pyroclastic flow, or great cloud of superheated gas and hot ash, rushed down the mountain like a raging river incinerating and covering everything in its path with several feet of ash. By the time the volcanic storm reached the town of Pompeii below, the ash had become a blinding blizzard of fine ash accelerating through the streets with lightning speed. People fleeing for their lives were instantaneously asphyxiated by the firestorm of fine ash and buried under several feet of ash and debris. Archeologists investigating the ruins years later found that they could make castings of the impressions of the bodies buried under the ash by filling the cavity with liquid plaster. The photograph illustrates the amazing detail of the casting of a victim who apparently died instantly in his futile attempt to escape death. Imagine the number of deaths that will result from the many violent eruptions of volcanoes similar to Vesuvius during the horrific invasion of earth.

A casting of a Pompeii victim
Photograph by J.E. Bouvier

DEADLY MISSILES

Most of us have learned not to say that things cannot get any worse in the middle of unfavorable circumstances because it can always get worse and sometimes does. While towns, cities and people are being buried by ash, John proceeded to describe meteors falling to earth from space like overripe figs thrown from a fig tree in a windstorm.[12] The remains or fragments of small meteors called meteorites have been a common sight in many places around the world for centuries and usually strike the earth causing little or no damage.

However, think for a moment about the effects of dozens, hundreds or even thousands of meteors massive enough to strike the earth's surface like the famous Barringer meteor. This meteor from outer space forged the best preserved crater on earth located about thirty minutes from Flagstaff, Arizona. The meteor struck the earth an estimated fifty thousand years ago. I saw this crater, which is quite a formidable hole in the desert floor, from an airplane 30,000 feet above the site. I tried to imagine the impact of the massive meteor as it came rocketing through the atmosphere from outer space. The meteor maintained enough of its mass to strike the desert floor and form a chasm "three fourths of a mile wide and 570 feet deep. The meteor itself has been estimated to be 150 feet wide and weigh 300,000 tons."[13] Imagine the explosion of sand and rock scattered over miles of desert from the impact with dust so thick you couldn't see for days. Anything located in the area where the meteor collided with the earth would have literally been vaporized from the impact. If a person had witnessed this massive meteor streaking across the sky with its flaming tail stretching miles skyward, he would surely have thought that the sky was falling.

"An estimated ten million rocky asteroids and ice-and-dirt comets pirouette in outer space, and once in awhile their paths fatefully intersect our planet's. One such encounter took place a hundred miles from present-day Washington D.C., where a 53-mile-wide crater lies buried beneath Chesapeake Bay-the scar left when a two-mile-wide rock smashed into the seafloor 35 million years ago. More notorious is the titan, six miles in diameter that barreled into the Gulf of Mexico around 65 million years ago, releasing thousands of times more energy than all the nuclear weapons on the planet combined. On June 30, 1908, an object the size of a 15 story building fell in a remote part of Siberia called Tunguska. The object-an asteroid or a small comet-exploded a few miles before impact, scorching and blowing down trees across 800 square miles."[14] This asteroid reportedly rocketed to earth at an estimated speed of more than 30,000 miles an hour.

Perhaps the impact of these historical meteors striking earth are just examples to illustrate what the world will experience when the massive chunks of space rock are suddenly and supernaturally diverted from their harmless trajectories and reprogrammed to strike targets on earth like deadly missiles. Try to imagine the chaos and panic that just one meteor, like the one that formed the crater in Arizona, would cause if it impacted downtown New York City at the height of the business day. Man with all his technology may indeed see the meteors approaching earth, but he will be helpless to stop the devastation from the impact of this galactic barrage. There have even been discussions among scientists about sending missiles to redirect the course of rogue meteors or asteroids heading toward our planet. In 2009 Russia embarked on a mission to launch missiles with explosive warheads to alter the course of the massive Apophis asteroid calculated to come dangerously close to earth in coming years. A similar plan worked in the world of fictionalized drama in the movie *Armageddon*. However, any attempt to stop the barrage of space missiles during the supernatural invasion of earth will be absolutely futile.

THE SANCTUARY

The destruction caused by the opening of the sixth seal will cause even the rich and famous, the great and mighty and the heads of nations to look in vain for a place to hide. In fact, in the midst of the chaos and mayhem, John observed people from all walks of life throughout the world rushing frantically to any subterranean opening that advertised the promise of protection from the deadly missiles rocketing to earth. Imagine millions of hysterical people attempting to squeeze into underground World War II bunkers and bomb shelters that were already crammed to capacity by those seeking shelter from the widespread destruction of World War III. Perhaps others will crowd into caves and deep caverns provided by nature like the mammoth Carlsbad Cavern in New Mexico as well as expansive catacombs throughout the world that served as tombs for the dead and tourist attractions for the living. John may have even witnessed multitudes of people flooding into a manmade cavernous expanse hollowed out of the Yucca Mountain located in southern Nevada.

This infamous project was conceived to be the only repository in the U.S. for the safe long-term storage of radioactive waste material remaining from fuel used to power some electrical generating plants. After considerable study and several billion dollars expended on the construction of a network of tunnels and cavernous rooms for storage of nuclear waste in the mountain, all work was suspended in 2010. Since nuclear waste was never deposited in the facility, scientists living during the invasion may quickly realize the mountain may be easily converted into a safe haven for mankind affording protection from radioactivity from nuclear blasts, earthquakes and even the barrage of space missiles. Imagine the following horrifying scenario as panic-stricken people battle a sea of humanity seeking refuge in the sanctuary of the mountain.

Soon after the invasion begins, the President of the New World Order (the Antichrist) will secretly expedite the modification of the mountain facility to a self-contained sanctuary capable of sustaining human life for an extended period of time. A top secret lottery system will be implemented to select and notify the exclusive future tenants of the facility that they have been selected to survive the invasion. However, due to limited space, only the names of the young, healthy and those with extraordinary intellectual attributes and skills necessary to maintain life in the sanctuary and later repopulate and rebuild the infrastructures of the earth will be included in the lottery.

The news of the sanctuary and the top secret process of selecting those to escape to the mountain refuge quickly leaks out to the media and spreads like a wildfire throughout the world. It seems like everyone has knowledge of the secret schedules and locations where government aircraft and vehicles will board waiting groups of people with valid lottery passes and transport them to the mountain. Overnight, violence in the streets escalates to a new level and a horrifying bloody scene erupts across the world in one city after another. Desperate people struggling to survive claw their way through crowds attempting to board vehicles and aircraft at the risk of being shot by members of the Antichrist's private army. Scores of innocent people are trampled and killed in the streets. Highways are jammed with frantic people determined to make their way to the sanctuary. Many of those with lottery passes are murdered and their

IDs sold to the highest bidder on the black market. Even as the sanctuary is crammed to capacity and the massive doors to the entrance slowly grind to a close with the frightened tenants safely inside breathing a sigh of relief, multitudes fight to squeeze through the ever-shrinking portal to safety. Unfortunately, this valiant effort to save mankind will be futile and life in the sanctuary will be short-lived as the invasion exacts its toll on the planet.

The Antichrist will likely continue to attribute the natural disasters and relentless bombardment of the earth by rogue rocks from space to the same invaders blamed for kidnapping the missing people. Although there is no indication as to who or what they are, where they are from or what they want, he will assure the population that he will find out and stop the attacks. It will also be necessary for the world leader to reinforce the fact that the strange occurrences can be explained and they are definitely not leading to the end of the world as predicted by some groups of people.

The opening of the six seals will unleash almost every conceivable weapon on mankind that the earth, heavens and galaxies can produce. I said almost every weapon because there are still some surprises for humanity. The next offensive of the invasion will bring even greater challenges and more astounding out-of-this-world weapons of mass destruction for the world's inhabitants.

REFLECTIONS

- There will be massive destruction on earth initiated by the opening of six seals.

- The first seal will quietly introduce the Antichrist as he takes the helm of the New World Order.

- The second seal will initiate relentless wars on the earth between and within nations.

- The third seal will introduce hyper-inflation that causes an escalation in famine and disease.

- The fourth seal will introduce a massive increase in deaths worldwide. Approximately 1.5 billion people will die as a result of the wars, famine, disease, and even attacks from rogue animals.

- The fifth seal is a departure from the destruction on earth and will take place in heaven. John was able to see the multitudes of people that accepted the gift of life during the invasion and died as martyrs.

- The sixth seal will introduce a great earthquake. The world will be plunged into darkness and the planet will be relentlessly bombarded by deadly meteors and asteroids.

11

THE GOOD, THE BAD, AND THE UGLY

*a*s the world reels from the devastation delivered by the opening of the first six seals of destruction, we are introduced to several groups of spiritual beings or visitors from another dimension apart from our world called angels. Although they will play a key role in the launch and execution of the final phases of the shocking invasion their existence and invisible presence on earth may be difficult to comprehend. However, it may surprise you to learn that not all angels are good nor do they all reside in heaven as often characterized in books and movies. Discover the real story behind the good, the bad, and the ugly angels and the critical responsibilities they will have during the invasion.

ANGELS

At one time all spiritual beings known as angels resided in heaven. However, as explained later a very special angel known as Satan rebelled against the God of the universe and was banned to earth along with legions of his wicked followers. These spirits became known as fallen angels or demons. You may find the following account of these wicked spirits to be somewhat unbelievable. That's exactly what they hope! Armed with diabolical powers and superhuman strength these evil spirits or demons are dangerous and are no match for frail humans. However, these vicious beings have different roles to play in the everyday drama of mankind and the invasion of earth depending on their level of malicious conduct. There are three groups of fallen angels.

The first group of demons is destined to roam the earth daily with Satan, their "prince of darkness." Their goal in life is to wreck every home and destroy every life possible, ultimately dragging the devastated souls to their lair in eternal darkness. The finished product of their handiwork on earth is evident everywhere. In fact, you may have had an encounter with one or more of these nasty spirits. However, since the presence of the vicious creatures is usually manifested only by subtle rogue thoughts planted in your mind, you would not have necessarily recognized their presence. Although the ancient manuscripts do not specify responsibilities for these evil spirits during the invasion, they will probably all be working day and night aggressively pursuing "business as usual."

The second group of four fallen angels will definitely play a critical role in the invasion. However, these demons were so vicious they were not permitted to freely roam the earth with the other demons. These four foul spirits which we must label the bad angels are supernaturally "chained" on earth near the Euphrates River in the Middle East until the appropriate time during the invasion when they will be released.

The third group of fallen angels consisting of legions of malicious, vile spirits apparently exhibited acts of evil so wicked that they are chained in darkness in a "bottomless pit." They are destined to live out their existence in shackles until the invasion begins and the time arrives for their release. They are the worst of the worst! At the proper moment in time, these unstoppable, ferocious, appalling demons will be released with an insatiable appetite to torture and kill those living on earth. We must refer to these atrociously evil demons of the dark side as the ugly angels. The responsibilities of the bad angels and the ugly angels during the invasion will be discussed in the next chapter.

THE GOOD ANGELS

The good angels still reside in heaven and have played an active role in the lives of people throughout history. We will simply refer to them as angels. Historically these angels routinely visited earth and shared prophecies of the future with men like Daniel. Yes, the strange messengers discussed earlier were some of the good angels. Even today these spiritual messengers routinely visit earth to intervene in our lives as invisible beings. Other times, they arrive disguised as ordinary people looking like any of us. When they do confront us, we often do not recognize them as angels. At times, they may appear to be strangers whom we have an opportunity to help. Remember the fellow on the street corner with the sign looking for a helping hand? It made you feel good to give the guy a little extra money and you thought it was coincidental that the rest of your day was strangely wonderful and without incident. What about the guy who said he needed a pair of shoes? Did you help?

> *The next time you're confronted by a stranger in need, remember he could be an angel sent to encourage you, help you through a difficult time or just add a little sunshine to your day.*

Following the opening of the six seals, seven special angels will embark on the most awesome supernatural task of all time, even for angels. Their mission will be to personally unleash the next seven stages of destruction on earth. The world will still be staggering from the recent onslaught of famine, war, disease and the physical abuse of nature resulting in the deaths of more than a billion people. Pandemonium and confusion will be rampant. People will be terrified of what will happen next. It will appear the world is hopelessly and madly spinning out of control.

QUIET PLEASE!

When the seventh seal was opened, there was complete silence in heaven for about thirty minutes.[1] All activity ceased! There are probably very few of us who have ever experienced complete silence for thirty minutes, unless we were asleep. We're not told why there will be silence in heaven. Perhaps it is the impact of the awesome devastation and loss of human life on earth during the opening of the first six seals. Those residing in heaven will be happy to see friends and relatives who were left after the evacuation of the "Chosen" accept the gift of life. They must now endure the invasion but at least they will escape a fate in eternity worse than death. Unfortunately, they may also witness the death of countless friends, family and co-workers who were left and who refused the gift of life. Even God will be saddened by the loss of the vast numbers of his creation who stand fast and stubbornly refuse to accept the gift. If only they knew what waits for them on the other side of the grave. It will be like watching helplessly as your own children refuse your pleading and repeated warnings of danger and then walk head on into a deadly experience that ultimately takes their lives and condemns them to a fate worse than death in eternity.

Everything possible will be done to encourage those left to accept the gift of life, but in the end it will be each individual's choice. Perhaps this brief period of silence will be for those in heaven to grieve for friends and loved ones who refused the gift.

> *We should all be grateful for the patience of God and his desire to see all mankind spared from the shocking deadly invasion of earth. If just one more person accepts the gift of life and survives the end of the world, it will be worth it all.*

THE SECOND OFFENSIVE

During the second offensive the sound of each of seven supernatural trumpets will announce the release of the next weapon of mass destruction.

THE SOUNDS OF TERROR

If you were living in the United States during the "cold war," you're familiar with the ominous drone of sirens every Friday at noon warning of an enemy attack. Of course, it was only a drill but the reverberating sound pierced the quietness of the day and sent chills down the backs of many who anticipated the "real thing" one day. I still remember crouching down in the hall outside of my elementary school classroom with my head in my lap impatiently waiting for the "all-clear" siren. The ancient manuscripts are not clear as to whether people on earth will hear the sounds of the supernatural trumpets announcing each destructive attack in the second offensive of the invasion. However, imagine that people will actually hear the earsplitting warning indicating the next weapon of mass destruction is "armed" and about to be launched toward earth. Of course there will be no place to hide and no "all-clear" siren. The anticipation of destruction will be enough to scare anyone. The blast of the trumpets will literally be the sounds of terror to those still living on earth!

A BLOCKBUSTER HORROR MOVIE

John watched as each of the seven special angels entrusted with a supernatural trumpet lined up and stood silently and patiently waiting for the signal to begin. The first trumpet sounded and immediately the atmosphere over the earth was saturated with hail and fire, mingled with blood.[2] As a result of this bizarre "rain," all the grass and one-third of all the trees on earth will be immediately destroyed.

There will be tremendous loss of property and lives due to the relentless pelting of hail and fire. Recall the damage from the forest fires that often frequent California, destroying lives, expensive homes and property and thousands of acres of forests. Imagine that kind of disaster multiplied by hundreds of millions of acres of uncontrolled fires raging throughout the world. The planet will literally be engulfed in choking smoke.

The loss of green grass, plants and trees will ultimately upset the balance of nature on earth. The natural conversion of carbon dioxide to oxygen by photosynthesis will be dramatically reduced, making it difficult for people and animals to breathe. There is no known chemical system that can serve as a substitute for this incredible natural process. Pollution will be rampant and the quality of air drastically deteriorated. People with asthma and other respiratory diseases will be dependent on bottled oxygen for survival.

There will be shortages of everything. All forms of fruits, vegetables, lumber for building materials, and feed for meat-producing animals like chickens and cattle will be in short supply. Later as the rains fall, erosion of the landscape due to the loss of trees and grass will cause dangerous mudslides unparalleled by anything in history. Finally, everything, including people, will be drenched in blood raining from the skies. Combine the polluted air, shortages of food and necessities and devastating damage due to the fires with the shocking psychological effects of blood drenching everyone and everything, and you have the script for a blockbuster horror movie. However, this drama will be very real.

TARGET EARTH

The second angel sounded his trumpet. John described what appeared to be a mammoth mountain burning with fire, plummeting from the sky into the sea.[3] Perhaps this is one of many asteroids speeding harmlessly through space that will be supernaturally redirected to target earth. Astronomers studying the galaxies will notice an asteroid that they previously predicted to pass a safe distance from earth's orbit abruptly and without scientific explanation changes course. They will be panic-stricken to see it unexpectedly rocketing on a collision course with earth. The world had already experienced the explosive impact of a shower of deadly meteors potentially striking major cities worldwide. Fortunately this massive space rock will make its impact in the ocean.

The enormous asteroid will enter the dense atmosphere of the earth and burn violently as portions of it vaporize due to friction with the air. When the rogue space rock finally smashes into the water, one-third of the sea will become blood, partly due to the destruction of fish and creatures in the sea. In addition, one-third of all the ships in the sea will be destroyed contributing the blood of their crew and passengers to the ocean. Vast numbers of people will die in this graphic presentation of disaster witnessed by John. He must have seen modern warships of great navies and the latest behemoth cruise ships with thousands of passengers destroyed in a few fleeting minutes. Our world has never experienced such a massive picture of destruction that will be realized by the impact of a single asteroid the size of a great mountain.

Several years ago my wife and I were on a cruise ship in the Mediterranean Sea. One day as I gazed out on the calm open sea and clear skies, I began to imagine the panic that will grip the heart of anyone watching when a massive flaming asteroid like the one described by John is seen suddenly rocketing toward earth from space. As the asteroid, perhaps the size of Mount St. Helens or Mount McKinley, rips through the atmosphere at thousands of miles an hour and speeds toward earth, I imagined you could see the blinding glow of light from the gigantic space rock's white hot molten surface. There will be a billowing white condensation trail mixed with flaming debris peeling off the massive rock stretching miles into the upper atmosphere. Clouds of dense smoke formed by the burning superheated gases exploding from the asteroid will blanket the sky. This is not a sight to be admired. A deadly shock wave generating hurricane-force winds will precede the asteroid hurtling toward earth at supersonic speed followed by the sound of a deafening explosion characteristic of a sonic boom. The world may have very little notice of the approaching disaster from those who study the stars and only the fortunate ones will be out of the strike zone where and when it collides with earth.

People will suddenly realize they will die from the colossal surge of water caused by the asteroid hitting the ocean if they're not killed by the direct impact of the rocky missile. Their minds may wander while their bodies are frozen in the few seconds remaining before the rogue space rock collides with the sea. Some people may realize they had written off the previous events of the invasion as coincidence or happenstance. They may have agreed with scientists that the events were just freaks of nature caused by unprecedented solar flares from the sun. Perhaps they embraced the report given by the President of the New World Order that the disasters were caused by mysterious invaders from outer space.

Could the countdown to the end of the world have actually started? If only they had listened to that one who warned them they too could have escaped this impending horrible death! The key to survival that they did not possess will be revealed later. That key will unlock the secret to surviving the end of the world. Meanwhile, a gigantic wall of steam will be generated at the surface of the sea seconds ahead of the flaming asteroid as it approaches the water. This superheated steam traveling outward from the point of impact will instantly boil every living thing in its path. Finally, everything in sight, dead or alive, will be sucked down to a watery grave in a powerful vortex formed by the asteroid plummeting to the ocean floor. However, the death and destruction from this asteroid is not over yet!

One of the world's largest ocean liners
Photograph by J.E. Bouvier

As the massive asteroid thrusts its way down through the water to the bottom of the ocean, a gigantic tidal wave will be generated. An enormous wall of water will rise up like a prehistoric sea monster reaching for the sky. Everything and everyone in its path for miles from the point of impact will be destroyed. It will produce a destructive wall of water right at the source radiating outwardly in all directions. Even ships like the massive ocean liner pictured will be tossed about like a child's bathtub toy. These vessels will be propelled effortlessly up the steep sides of the gigantic wall of water, and then dropped unmercifully down the side, becoming crushed by the impact of tons of water.

MISSILE FROM SPACE

On cue the third angel released the next phase of destruction by sounding his trumpet. John saw what looked like a flaming torch falling from the sky that is evidently another enormous meteorite or asteroid.[4] This missile from space will strike the earth in a strategic location where it will poison the watershed of one-third of the rivers. As a result, everyone dependent on water from these rivers must now look elsewhere for fresh water. In addition, many will be killed or injured from the explosive impact of the asteroid. The astronomers and scientists of the world, who are among the most intelligent people on earth, will realize they are powerless to stop this massive unnatural cosmic attack from deep space. Of course the infamous world leader may assert that there is evidence of a biological poison that was carried by the meteor and dispersed into the water. He may also claim that the invaders responsible for the unexplained disappearance of people must also be responsible for this attack on the water supply. The minds of the brightest people on earth will be focused on how the mysterious invaders are orchestrating this attack rather than listening to those who offer the secret to survival.

SUN, MOON AND STARS

The fourth angel created havoc on earth by sounding his trumpet and commanding the heavenly bodies of light in the solar system to make significant changes to their features.[5] The light from the sun that regulates our seasons and provides energy for the growth of crops will be diminished by approximately thirty-three percent. One-third of the moon that lights the night sky and controls our tides will be darkened while the light from one-third of the stars will be totally eliminated. People will be panic-stricken by the sudden unexplained changes in light from the heavenly bodies. The productivity of crops will be adversely affected, significantly reducing the already scarce food supply. This supernatural change in the heavenly bodies may even manifest itself by increasing the rotational speed of the earth and reducing the 24 hour day to 16 hours. The world will be absolutely baffled at how this can be happening and who has the power to make such astronomical adjustments to the solar system while maintaining it in perfect balance. Then John heard an angel flying through the heavens saying in a loud voice, "Woe" to the inhabitants of the earth. When you see the word "woe" in the ancient manuscripts, it means whoa! You haven't seen anything yet!

At this point in the invasion, everything man depends upon to sustain life on earth will have been negatively impacted by the relentless discharge of supernatural weapons of mass destruction. The earth will have been unmercifully bombarded by asteroids, rained on by meteors, fire and hail and literally cracked open by unprecedented earthquakes. Scientific equipment may indicate that the rotation of the earth is unstable validating ancient predictions that the earth will be rendered dangerously out of balance. Even the sun, moon and stars will take on an unnatural look that defies explanation and causes unsustainable mental trauma among the population. Food will be in short supply, the air will be contaminated and water supplies will be polluted. Rationing of necessities will become a way of life. Riots will become common occurrences as people fight among themselves for survival. Every home that stockpiled food, water and supplies, as well as firearms and ammunition prior to the invasion will become a target for starving, struggling people resorting to violence to survive.

Many who embrace the alien invasion and body-snatching theories may continue to give the aliens credit for being able to somehow harness the power of the celestial bodies in the solar system and use them as weapons of mass destruction against the earth. Astronomers will frequently scan the heavens looking for signs of alien spaceships parked in distant orbits that could be responsible for orchestrating this horrific attack on earth. Some scientists may even try to contact the invaders to plead for mercy for the earth and its inhabitants. Some industrialized nations may even prepare to launch rockets into space to destroy the invaders once they are discovered. Astronauts in the international space station will constantly monitor the devastation on earth as well as the vast reaches of space for evidence of intruders. Eventually, their safe vantage point in earth orbit will also concede to death and destruction, perhaps from a single stray meteor.

> *While ignoring its own destiny, mankind is totally infatuated with unidentified flying objects and the search for alien life-forms on other planets.*

The supernatural invasion approaches the mid-point of seven years. The Antichrist, firmly entrenched in his world leadership position, will continue his strategy to reach out and comfort the hurting world. He will offer help, peace, and security in the face of the mounting devastation of the invasion. He will also continue to blame the elusive invaders and natural phenomenon like solar flares on the sun for the destruction of earth and the suffering and death of so many people. The world leader will insist on finding a way to prevent further attacks. In so doing, he will strengthen his popularity and intensify his seduction of the panic-stricken population. However, the invasion of earth is about to escalate as a frightening army of diabolical beings arrive to terrorize the population.

REFLECTIONS

- The seventh seal is a break from the devastation on earth and describes a scene in heaven where there will be thirty minutes of uninterrupted silence.

- The sound of the first trumpet will cause fire and hail to rain down on the earth resulting in one-third of all the trees and green grass to be burned.

- The sound of the second trumpet will result in a massive asteroid being hurtled into the sea resulting in one-third of the sea turning to blood.

- The sound of the third trumpet will cause another enormous asteroid or meteor to fall to earth and poison one-third of the rivers and waterways reducing the drinking water supply for mankind.

- The sound of the fourth trumpet will darken one-third of the light from the sun, moon and stars.

12

THE "DARK SIDE"

The expression "it's going to be hell on earth" is used to describe a situation expected to be extremely difficult or impossible to manage. This often-used flippant phrase will become a sobering reality when people experience the next two weapons of mass destruction initiated by the sounds of the fifth and sixth trumpets. By this time, the world will be in total chaos from the crippling, deadly impacts of the previous supernatural bombardments from outer space, the devastation from conventional as well as nuclear war, worldwide famine, disease and natural disasters. However, the planet will now be subjected to an attack from the kind of malicious, terrorizing creatures that have only existed in science fiction movies made for harmless entertainment. At this time, hordes of powerful alien-like residents of the "dark side" of a supernatural dimension unknown to mankind will be unleashed on the earth. This assault will definitely not be a time for the faint-hearted and those with a low threshold for pain.

THE UGLY ANGELS

John witnessed a star falling to earth and saw an angel give "him" the key to the bottomless pit. Since John referred to the star as "him," we can conclude he saw a personality, not an object. Satan was the star or special angel who fell from heaven in early eternity; therefore, the star John saw must be Satan.[1] The sound of the fifth trumpet will signal the angel that it's time to give Satan the key and allow him to release legions of hideous demons who have been locked in the "bottomless pit" waiting centuries for this moment.

John gives us an incredibly detailed description of the creatures that emerged from the smoke in the pit. Although the demons are invisible spiritual beings, these creatures will more than likely take on a visible manifestation worthy of their diabolical makeup in order to intensify the shock value to their human victims. Their presence will be much more terrifying if people can see them. John called them locusts since they must have resembled insects with which he had some familiarity.[2] He said the shapes of the demons were like horses prepared for battle. In other words the locust-like creatures must have been covered with what looked like protective armor as were the Roman steeds used in battle with which John was familiar. John described the creatures as having faces like men, teeth like lions, hair like women and the sound of their wings was like chariots with horses running to battle. They had breastplates like iron and tails like scorpions. What a terrifying description! The ferocious looking creatures even had crowns on their heads that looked like gold. John did his best to describe these beings by saying they looked like things with which he was familiar. The description of these alien-looking creatures may remind us of science fiction movies made in the 1950's that depicted the invasion of earth by "giant insects," mutated by exposure to radiation from the underground testing of nuclear bombs.

Can you imagine coming face to face on a dark night with the locust-like creatures John described?

The description of their teeth and the sight of the poisonous stinger of torment in their tails will surely intimidate the toughest of fragile humans. Their agility and speed of flight produced by their powerful wings will make it almost impossible for the earthlings to escape their assailants. These demonic beings will look like something out of a frightening science fiction movie, except they will be shockingly real.

It is tempting to interpret this description of creatures to be modern attack helicopters with human pilots but John said the locust-like beings have a "king" over them called the angel of the bottomless pit. His name is Apollyon. Therefore, the commander of this vast legion of dauntless spirits is in charge of the bottomless pit and the devilish creatures which reside there. Clearly then, these imprisoned beings are the ugly angels who were cast out of heaven along with Satan and have been bound in chains of darkness until the time of the invasion.[3]

We must pause here for a moment to note that the demonic salesmen of evil will unknowingly be used in a mysterious way to encourage mankind to accept the gift of life before it's too late. God will use the powers of darkness to literally scare and torture mankind into submission. Since time is short, anything that will save mankind from a fate worse than death is fair. Evil has often been used to provide a wake-up call for mankind. I believe we saw a vivid example of this in the United States with the terrorist attack on 9/11. Did we get the message?

The manuscripts omit a detailed description of the spectacular scene when the lock is opened and the demons are released from the pit to begin their attack, but imagine the following possible terrifying scenario.

At the sound of the fifth trumpet, Satan will snatch the key from the angel and eagerly open the lock. The doors to the pit will burst open from the pressure of the shoving and pushing of the agitated demons. These creatures have been imprisoned since early eternity, and they will struggle wildly and impatiently to make their escape from the abyss. They will scramble to the top of the opening and finally escape into the freedom of the skies. The opening of the pit will belch thick, hot, smoke from deep in the bowels of the earth and the stench of sulfur will permeate the air. It seems the demonic alien-looking creatures will never stop boiling out of the open pit as they straighten their wings and take flight to pursue unsuspecting victims. The smoke will block the light of the sun and the heavens will grow dark with millions of demonic winged beings streaming across the horizon. The noise from the sound of the wings of legions of demons beating their way to freedom will be deafening and drown out the sounds of nearby victims already screaming in vain for help.

The demons will be instructed to attack and torment for five months only those people without a seal of protection in their foreheads. Oh yes, those that accept the gift of life during the invasion will have a visible, identifying mark or "tattoo" on their foreheads that will protect them from these invaders. All others will be prime targets for the demons. Evidently only the demonic invaders and those who have accepted the gift of life will be able to see the mark of protection.

The creatures will be specifically instructed not to kill their victims. Why? They would love to torment their prey and then finish them off. This period of insurmountable pain without relief is to strongly encourage mankind to accept the gift of life. Perhaps the throbbing pain will be the catalyst required for many to make a decision while there is still time. The agony of this pain will be so horrible that some people will try to commit suicide but they will not be able to die, not yet! The Antichrist will do everything in his power to stop the vicious attack of the creatures but his efforts will be in vain. The weapons of the military will be useless against the supernatural power of the alien-like demons. Scientists may conclude these creatures are the invaders responsible for the destruction of earth and begin to diligently search for their spacecraft.

THE BAD ANGELS

The approximate end of the first half of the invasion

John heard a voice from heaven instructing the sixth angel to sound his trumpet and release the four bad angels bound at the great Euphrates River, which has always held a prominent place in history. The fact that these four angels have been imprisoned since Satan fell from heaven indicates they are more vicious than the legions of demons who roam the earth today but not bad enough to be restrained in the bottomless pit with the ugly angels. Imagine their relentless desire over the centuries to participate in Satan's evil work. From their prison these demons witnessed the first murder, the building of the tower of Babel and the construction of the idolatrous city of Babylon on the banks of the Euphrates River. In recent years they witnessed the ruthless rule and murderous acts of Saddam Hussein as he massacred his own people in Iraq until he was recently tried for his criminal acts and executed.

At the sound of the sixth trumpet, the chains of the four demons will be broken and they will be free for approximately thirteen months.[4] They will gather a supernatural army 200 million strong to attack, torment and kill the frightened people remaining on earth. It's a known fact that China has boasted of having an army of 200 million trained military personnel. However, John described an army of horses and saw breastplates of fire and brimstone on those riding the horses. In this instance, John didn't say they looked like horses; he said they were horses. He said the heads of the horses were like the heads of lions, and they had tails like serpents. John also saw fire, smoke and brimstone coming from the mouths of the horses.

It would be exciting to interpret these creatures to be modern-day war machines, rocket launchers or an army of 200 million military personnel. However, the description sounds more like demonic life-forms similar to the ugly angels John previously described. They will set out to kill an additional one-third of the remaining population of the earth with fire, smoke and brimstone from their mouths. Think about that! There will be 200 million sinister alien-like beings who will roam the earth with the look and smell of death. To put it in perspective, that's an army the size of two-thirds the entire population of the United States in 2010.

Mankind doesn't stand a chance. Their puny weapons will be totally useless against the supernatural powers of darkness. The world may speculate this is another massive alien attack intended to eradicate all life on earth. Scientists will be bewildered that there is absolutely no sign of any kind of craft that brought the disgusting invaders to the planet. Where did they come from and who are they? Homes, businesses and factories will be invaded and overrun, and innocent people will be ruthlessly slaughtered throughout the world. The landscape around the world will be littered with bodies, too many for anyone to take care of properly. Life will seem hopeless!

Recall that one-fourth of the earth's population or approximately 1.5 billion people will be killed during the opening of the first six seals. One-third of the remaining population will be murdered by the evil alien-like invaders. That means there will be an additional 1.5 billion people killed (based on 4.5 billion people living at the time) or more than three billion people total. There is no way to comprehend that astonishing death toll or the complications it brings to maintaining any semblance of life on earth. The critical infrastructure of the world will be dismantled further by the massive number of deaths. Of course, the Antichrist will propose one plan after another to address the escalating turmoil and panic in the world but to no avail. It will only get worse!

By the halfway point in the invasion it will seem that mankind has been exposed to almost every type of devastating attack imaginable to compel him to accept the gift of life including legions of vicious demons that alone destroyed more than a billion people. During this time there will be thousands of people who gracefully receive the gift and will be protected from further demon attacks. However, John noticed that many of those who survived the deadly attack of the demons still stubbornly refused to accept the only way to escape the fate worse than death. There is no better example of the vain, stubbornness, and selfishness of mankind than the people who will die needlessly during the horrible invasion and spend eternity tormented in darkness.

REFLECTIONS

Reflect on what the people still living after the evacuation of the "Chosen" will have experienced in the first forty-two months of the invasion. This will be approximately the halfway point in the invasion.

- The opening of the first seal will introduce the Antichrist as he takes the helm of the New World Order.

- The opening of the second seal will remove the constraints on mankind to go to war. Relentless wars on the earth between and within nations will begin and the threat of nuclear aggression will become a reality.

- The opening of the third seal will introduce famine and disease throughout the world.

- The opening of the fourth seal will cause approximately 1.5 billion people to die as a result of the wars, famine and disease.

- The opening of the fifth seal will be a departure from the assault on earth and take place in heaven. John saw the multitudes of people who died because of their acceptance of the gift of life during the invasion.

- The opening of the sixth seal will initiate a great earthquake and cause the world to be plunged into darkness. This seal also initiates the bombardment of the earth by meteors and asteroids.

- The opening of the seventh seal is another departure from the devastation on earth and describes a scene in heaven where there will be thirty minutes of uninterrupted silence.

- The sound of the first trumpet will cause fire and hail to rain down on the earth resulting in one third of all the trees and green grass being destroyed.

- The sound of the second trumpet will result in a massive asteroid being hurtled into the sea resulting in one-third of the sea turning to blood.

- The sound of the third trumpet will cause another enormous asteroid or meteor to fall to earth and poison one-third of the rivers and waterways thus reducing the supply of drinking water for mankind.

- The sound of the fourth trumpet will darken one-third of the light from the sun, moon and stars.

- The sound of the fifth trumpet will unleash a new weapon on mankind, alien-like creatures from the dark side to torture only those who have not accepted the gift of life.

- The sound of the sixth trumpet will release 200 million alien-like demonic beings which will result in the death of one-third of the remaining population on earth. This will bring the death toll during the global invasion to more than three billion people or approximately fifty percent of the population of the world remaining after the evacuation of the "Chosen."

13

LAST CALL

---

*a*t the midpoint of the seven-year-long invasion, the Antichrist will experience a diabolical metamorphosis that transforms him from a world leader to a brutal dictator. His initial agenda to control the world will be broadened to steal the most prized possession of every living person. His ultimate quest will be to seduce them into surrendering their very soul in exchange for the promise of a better life on earth. When they agree to the "deal," they will unknowingly seal their fate for all eternity in the darkness of his abode. Therefore, after all other means to communicate the message of hope to the world have been exhausted a supernatural effort will be made to ensure every single person has been offered the gift of life at least one time before it's too late. Also, every person will be given a clear understanding of the consequences of the "deal" that the Antichrist is offering. This last call to mankind will reach the entire population of the world with the message of hope.

AN ARMY OF MESSENGERS

Immediately after the "Chosen" is evacuated from the earth, there will be no one left who possesses the gift of life, although many will have some knowledge of the book that contains the key to the secret. It would seem almost "criminal" to leave mankind wandering aimlessly on the earth completely void of hope in the midst of panic and turmoil with certain death waiting around every corner. The current vacuum of despair would also leave the remaining population an easy prey to the seductive clutches of the Antichrist.

John suddenly experienced a flashback to the beginning of the invasion shortly after the evacuation of the "Chosen." Many people who were familiar with the gift of life but refused to accept it will finally realize the countdown to the end of the world has actually started. They will desperately search for the book where the key to the gift of life is concealed. After discovering and accepting the gift themselves they will become excited committed promoters of the message to others. The recent bizarre unexplained disappearance of the masses of people will validate the truth of the warning they found in the insider information provided by the ancient manuscripts. Therefore, a supernatural army of messengers will rise up out of those who are left and offer the key to the secret of the gift to anyone who will listen. John saw an angel that was responsible for identifying and protecting the new couriers of the message with an elite mark. He heard the angel say there were 144,000 people in this new army of messengers.[1]

THE TIME TRAVELERS

In addition to the army of 144,000 messengers, there will be another secret weapon to deter the Antichrist in his mission to snatch the souls of the remaining population. Two men from a past dimension in time will mysteriously materialize in the city of Jerusalem near the beginning of the invasion and turn Israel upside down for three-and-one-half years.[2] They will describe the dreadful suffering and death still to come and compel the Jews to accept the gift of life before it's too late. The men will urge the people to reject the empty promises of the Antichrist and avoid his diabolical trap.

These two time travelers will arrive with supernatural powers to enable them to stop the rain, turn water to blood and cause plagues on the earth in order to capture the attention of mankind and ensure their mission on earth is a success. The ancient manuscripts predict any man who attempts to harm the two prophets before their mission is complete will be destroyed by supernatural fire from the two men. As a result of the work of these two messengers approximately one-third of the population of Israel will accept the gift of life and escape a deadly surprise attack by the Antichrist later in the invasion.

THE AWAKENING

John's focus on the two men in Jerusalem was interrupted and his attention was diverted back to heaven. John saw a great multitude of people in heaven from all nations and languages too numerous to count. They were clothed in white robes with palm branches in their hands. Then one of the beings in heaven asked John if he knew who the people in the white robes were and where they came from. John didn't recognize any of the people since they were all from the future. The being explained these people accepted the gift of life during the invasion and later died as martyrs as a result of that decision.[3] Their changed lives were a stumbling block to the agenda of the Antichrist, and he had them executed. Therefore, after being murdered the spirits of these people were supernaturally transported to heaven where they will reside for all eternity.

This transformation of lives by the gift of life during the invasion may be the largest ingathering of heaven-bound people in the history of the world. The population of the world has grown slowly during the last two thousand years but very quickly in the last fifty years. There have been less than a billion people on the planet in any one year until about 1800. It's only been in the last fifty years that the population of the world has skyrocketed from approximately 2.4 billion in 1950 to the current population of more than 6.7 billion and of course it is still growing at an explosive rate.[4] Therefore, more people may discover the gift of life during the short seven years of the invasion than in all the centuries combined since the birth of the "Chosen" almost 2,000 years ago. You see, the dreaded invasion of the planet is all part of the master plan to compel the maximum number of people in the world to discover and accept the gift of life before they die.

Now we know that heaven is the final destination for all members of the "Chosen" as well as all others who accept the amazing gift of life during the invasion. These eternal residents of heaven are often referred to as saints.

THE "MIDNIGHT HOUR"

John saw another angel emerge on cue from the crowd of heavenly beings. As the Antichrist prepares to intensify his diabolical quest for the souls of mankind, a special angel will embark on a supernatural mission trip around the entire world. This angel with mystical powers will deliver a simple message of hope to every single person in every city in every country and in every language.[5] What an awesome responsibility this angel will have. Everyone will at least hear and understand the message of the gift of life one time.

How will the angel reach everyone before the world ends? The angel may use supernatural means although the day is coming when almost every person may have access to a television, computer, cell phone or other personal electronic device which could be used to receive the message! However, the angel is only the messenger and the choice will still be up to each individual.

John saw a second angel leave heaven and follow the first one. The second angel will warn the world that the ecumenical or "fashionable counterfeit religion" that so many chose to worship in pursuit of pleasure and worldly possessions has been destroyed by the Antichrist (discussed later). Their presumed entitlement of a path to heaven promised by the trendy religion was always an empty promise. The gift of life is their only hope. Then a third angel emerges with an awesome but grave responsibility. He will proclaim a warning of a fate worse than death for anyone refusing the message delivered by the first angel and choosing to follow the Antichrist. This angel promises eternity with torment by fire and brimstone in the abode of darkness for those who ultimately reject the gift. This may seem like a bizarre and unbelievable retribution for refusing the gift but it's true.

Following two more attacks on earth announced by the fifth and sixth trumpets, an angel will abruptly announce there is no more time! He will proclaim that when the seventh angel sounds his trumpet, the mystery will be finished. The gift that can alter the future of mankind has always been a great mystery and will never be completely understood! When the three angels complete their mission of mercy, it will be the "midnight hour" and the population of the earth will have heard the last call to accept the gift of life. Of course, people will still be able to make a decision to accept the gift any time until they draw their last breath, but they will not receive another reminder. However, during the last three-and-one-half years of the invasion, the Antichrist will make it almost impossible for a person to accept the gift. You won't believe what this diabolical fiend has up his sinister sleeve. One thing for sure, it's gonna get ugly!

REFLECTIONS

- Soon after the invasion begins, an army of 144,000 messengers will be gathered from those who accept the gift of life to spread the simple message of the gift to the world.

- Two time travelers from a past dimension will be sent to Jerusalem to supplement the work of the 144,000 messengers.

- There will be a great spiritual awakening during the invasion. It's likely that more people will accept the gift of life during the horrible invasion of earth than in all the years since the birth of the "Chosen" almost 2,000 years ago.

- A special angel will make one last trip around the world to ensure every person has heard the simple message of the gift of life one time before the end comes.

- A second angel will warn the world that the false ecumenical religion has been destroyed.

- A third angel will ensure every person has heard the consequences of refusing the gift of life and accepting the offer of the Antichrist.

14

IT'S GONNA GET UGLY!

*Y*ears ago I took our son to a small tent circus near our home where we had front-row seats for the opening performance. The grand finale was a magician who promised to make a live tiger vanish from a cage and then reappear in an empty cage about fifty feet away. Both cages were suspended in the air so no one could help the tiger change places. Dark blankets were draped over the cages to hide the contents from our view while the magician uttered a few unintelligible words and waved his "magic" wand. When the blankets were removed, the tiger had actually moved from one cage to the other. You could hear the audience gasping in absolute amazement. The world loves a good magic trick. To this day, we have no idea how the magician performed that feat. It was just a trick, some kind of "sleight of hand," but it was amazing!

About the mid-point of the invasion of earth, the world will witness the greatest performance of magic in history, but this will be real magic, demonic magic! The Antichrist's unforgettable performance of a lifetime will electrify the world and it promises to scare the life out of anyone that's there to witness it!

Meanwhile, John took time out from documenting the horrible invasion on earth to describe a mysterious war erupting in the heavens. It may be impossible to comprehend this next chronicle of events because it takes place beyond the world of mortals in a timeless spiritual dimension that cannot be explained by facts, logic or any form of scientific justification. John experienced a flashback that spanned a time before mankind arrived on the earth and continued through the mid-point of the invasion climaxing with an unbelievable war in the heavens. The outcome of this war will produce the catalyst that drives the Antichrist to Armageddon dragging the destiny of the human race with him.

The beginning of the second half of the invasion or the last 42 months

EVICTED

People often wonder where the subtle thoughts and feelings come from urging them to make decisions that could lead to crisis, heartache and even the destruction of their personal and family lives. To appreciate the origin of these powerful sensations that people experience, we must travel back in time with John. The narrative of his flashback in time began with a description of a scene in early eternity when all of heaven was in harmony, perfect harmony. Then an angel named Satan believed he deserved a position above all the other angels, as well as the God of the universe. He was determined to exalt himself above God and take what he believed was his rightful place as god of heaven and earth.

Satan was likely a very special angel and was referred to as the "son of the morning" in the ancient manuscripts.[1] Apparently he was the star of heaven. He lived a perfect existence up to this point and had everything he could possibly desire except the ultimate power of God, the Creator of the universe. However, Satan purposely defied the authority of God in his attempt to usurp His authority and therefore, he had to face the consequences.

> *Perhaps Satan had the same unquenchable obsession with position and power that many people have today. Simply put, he just wanted what he didn't have. Apparently, he wasn't any different than people today who are never satisfied with who they are, what they look like, what they have or where they're going.*

The harmony in heaven was temporarily interrupted when Satan was reprimanded for his ultimate act of disobedience. He was cast out of heaven destined to roam the earth and the airways. However, one-third of all of the angels in heaven actually applauded Satan's desire to be a god and supported him in his quest for power. They must have believed Satan had a shortcut to success and the ultimate power and position they too desired. As a result, God banned them all to earth and prepared a special place of torment in eternity for Satan and all the angels that followed him as the ultimate penalty for their disobedience. However, Satan and his followers will not face their punishment in eternity until after the conclusion of the invasion of earth.

Evicted from heaven, Satan and his fallen angels eagerly took on the distinct personality of formidable demonic spiritual beings with all the powers of darkness and superhuman strength at their command. Satan became the "prince of darkness" with the earth as his playground, promising equality of destruction to everyone on earth. Working with his demons, Satan has enjoyed seducing people for centuries, convincing them to defy all authority with the ultimate goal of destroying lives. After all, what could be more exciting than to destroy the lives of the very creatures that God created? However, Satan knows that in order to be successful, he must be subtle and cunning. Therefore, he plants subconscious but powerfully seductive thoughts, feelings and temptations in the minds and hearts of mankind urging them to lie, cheat, steal and murder as well as to commit all manner of other improper acts. He promises power, money, fame and endless pleasure but delivers only chains of hopelessness, pain, distress, and a fate in eternity worse than death.

Satan's hope is that people will always think of him only as a myth, a legend or a daunting apparition fictionalized as a humorous imaginary cartoon character in a red suit with horns and a long tail. In this way the deadly, diabolical agenda of Satan and his fiendish demons to destroy lives and steal the souls of unsuspecting people will remain a well-kept secret from the naive and gullible human race. We must be vigilant because these demons, as well as their leader Satan, are always stalking their prey. Mankind cannot possibly comprehend the diabolical strength of the "prince of darkness" and doesn't stand a chance against the demons' evil powers.

Even though Satan was cast out of heaven, he still has access to God. Interestingly enough, Satan is free to go back and forth to God to discuss the lives of mankind any time.[2] He appears in heaven daily accusing us of crimes against the Creator and petitioning God to punish us. Near the mid-point of the invasion, Satan will launch a final campaign with the help of all his fiendish demons to challenge God and the legions of angels in heaven once again for control of heaven, the earth and its inhabitants. The two sides will likely exercise supernatural powers unknown to mortal men in their battle against each other. In the end, the forces of good will prevail and Satan and his demons will be cast out of heaven for the second time, and this time, permanently. You can almost hear those in heaven saying "Good riddance! And on the way out, shut the door behind you." Satan and his demons will be confined to the earth for the balance of the invasion. John heard those in heaven rejoicing over the victory, but realizing the fury of Satan, they said, "Woe to those on earth."

After his second embarrassing defeat in heaven, Satan will call on all the spiritual demons of darkness and powers of evil at his command to rally about him and retaliate against God. Who should be his primary target for revenge? What about the nation of Israel? They have always been God's chosen people, His favorites. After all, it was Israel who gave birth to Jesus, the archenemy of Satan, more than 2,000 years ago. This will be about the time the Antichrist will break the treaty with Israel.

Before pursuing the Jews, Satan has an appointment with the Antichrist to discuss plans for his upcoming electrifying performance to the world. Together they will reveal the world's most diabolical plot ever imagined against the human race. John's heart must have been pounding as he listened intently to Satan hatching his evil plan to support the Antichrist in his ultimate takeover of the world and the final demise of mankind.

THE PERFORMANCE OF A LIFE TIME

Back on earth, the horrific invasion will intensify with no sign of relief. The once-pristine reputation of the Antichrist as a popular world leader will definitely be tarnished and in jeopardy due to the deteriorating condition of the planet. People will lose confidence in him and the government supporting him. The world he promised to restore and to rid of war is in shambles with more fighting than ever. The attack of the invaders is strengthening and people are dying by the millions. The world leader must act promptly before he completely loses his grasp on the world. Initially, people followed the Antichrist because they admired, respected and trusted him. Now he will need to command absolute obedience out of fear and make that fear dangerously real and personal, fear brought about by the actions of a ruthless dictator. Therefore, the Antichrist will stage a spectacular performance that will shock the world, convince everyone he is not one to be reckoned with and return him to his pedestal of absolute power.

Satan, who will actually orchestrate the theatrical act of the Antichrist, will make it as dramatic as possible to maximize the impact on the world. Since the manuscripts do not reveal the details of how this diabolical plan is executed, imagine the following scenario describing how the performance may take place.

The Antichrist (President of the New World Order) will arrange a meeting of presidents, heads of state, kings and queens, somewhere in Europe near his headquarters, a world summit. The purpose of the meeting will be to assess the eroding state of the world's infrastructures and failing economies due to the escalating invasion. He will discuss his plans to accelerate the recovery of the world from the deepening global crisis and unveil a strategy to stop the invaders from destroying the planet. Such a critical meeting with the world leader will attract representatives of the media worldwide and draw the interest of the general population. Of course, the proceedings of the summit will be televised live to the world because everyone will anticipate hearing the world leader's speech.

To symbolize the Antichrist's power, strength, stability and authority, the legendary meeting will be held in a stately, medieval European setting perhaps like the Windsor Castle in England. The world leader will give his speech from a room decorated with a vast assortment of medieval armor and battle gear such as knives, shields and swords. Of course, as a routine security measure, metal detectors will be strategically placed at the entrance of the castle to screen all attendees for potential weapons.

The Windsor Castle in England
Photograph by J.E. Bouvier

As the heads of state, invited guests and members of the media file into the building an assassin slips through the tight security and passes safely through the metal detectors. He poses as a member of the media with the appropriate security clearance. He carries no weapon and seemingly is not a threat to the president. Sometime during the president's speech, the assassin quietly leaves his seat and moves unnoticed to the front of the room where the president is speaking. The floor in front of the podium is crowded with anxious reporters. Under the pretense of taking the "perfect photo" of a significant moment in world history, the assassin moves even closer to the Antichrist and leans against a nearby wall decorated with antiquities of war.

While everyone's attention is fixed upon the world leader and his every word, the assassin reaches for a medieval sword hanging on the wall. In one swift motion, he retrieves the antique but razor-sharp sword, slashes at the head of the Antichrist and brandishes a deadly blow.[3] The security personnel leap over the crowd of people to apprehend the assassin but they immediately realize it's too crowded to use their weapons and it's too late. The Antichrist suddenly drops to the floor in a pool of blood with an unbelievable gash cut across his neck, his head practically severed from his body. You can almost hear the gasps of people around the world as they watch their messiah fall lifelessly to the floor right before their eyes on live television. Security and medical personnel quickly move the body to a secure area while those who apprehended the assassin take him into custody. The world has already been decimated by attacks from unknown invaders for more than three years and now the only person they believed capable of saving the world has been assassinated.

The assailant is removed from the premises while emergency personnel on standby rush to the aid of the stricken president. Within minutes, the attending physician somberly emerges from the secluded area where the body was taken. He walks slowly to a microphone and sadly pronounces to the world that their president is dead.

The closed casket of the Antichrist will lie in state prior to his burial, allowing mourners from around the world to express their admiration and respect for this great statesman. The rest of the world will watch via live television. As the lines of dignitaries and other mourners are still wrapped around the rotunda where the world leader lies in repose, suddenly and unexpectedly, something absolutely bizarre occurs literally shocking the world!

A mysterious transparent black cloud of vapor resembling the ghostly form of a man suddenly materializes in the room, glides silently through the air and hovers momentarily over the casket. Then the vaporous form is suddenly sucked right through the top of the casket. As absolute silence falls over the room, the latches click open on the casket and the lid begins to move, slowly at first, and then it swings wide open. Everyone's eyes are riveted on the body in the casket. Then the world leader slowly sits up and his eyes open. He glares at the crowd with a gaze burning like coals of fire. The crowd gasps as they repeatedly whisper, "He's alive," "He's alive." There will be no denying the fact that the Antichrist has been healed and has returned to life.[4] As the electricity of supernatural power begins to course throughout his body, the Antichrist moves gradually, first placing his hands over the side of the casket. As the television cameras quickly zoom in on him, he gazes around at the stunned crowd of people and slowly climbs out of the casket. He casually brushes himself off and stands to his feet, hesitating for a moment to regain his composure. His movements are a little stilted at first. You may be thinking, "How does this happen? Wasn't he embalmed?"

When the Antichrist dies, Satan will provide the supernatural power to resurrect his spirit from the bottomless pit where he has been residing since his death.[5] Recall that this is the place of imprisonment for the ugly angels and Apollyon their ghoulish king. After his death, the world leader will no longer be just a powerful, charismatic politician and world ruler. The Antichrist will be transformed into a demon-possessed, spiritual being looking like a human but possessing the same supernatural power as Satan.

The spectators in the room, as well as the entire world watching by television, are absolutely stunned and shocked in disbelief. Miraculously, the great leader appears to be healthier and stronger than ever. As the television cameras zoom in for a closer look at the resurrected leader, there are no visible wounds. When the Antichrist begins to speak, his once charismatic demeanor, accented by his smooth, reassuring words, is now the manifestation of a brutal tyrant with a defiant voice, a fierce look and eyes flashing evil. He boasts proudly of his god-like powers and vows to continue his rule to save the world from the invaders from space. News commentators and medical personnel vow to the world that this is no illusion, it's not a trick. They report that they personally witnessed his assassination and saw him die. He was pronounced dead by the medical examiner, and now he is definitely alive!

The world will be totally mesmerized by the resurrection of the Antichrist and will worship the transformed world leader and his demonstration of supernatural power.[6] People will believe he must be a god! After all, the world has always hungered for a visible, tangible god to worship, a king who rules the earth and will eliminate the requirement for faith. With such incredible power, he cannot be defeated by anyone. Surely this man of power will be able to defeat whoever is orchestrating the terrible invasion of earth. The Antichrist will boast of the source of his power and Satan worship will be revitalized.

The Antichrist is poised to commence the final stages of his rule of the world as a brutal, evil dictator with an agenda fueled by the power of Satan himself. The Minister of Propaganda introduced earlier will immediately put a fantastic global political spin on the resurrection of the Antichrist and the agenda of the revived world ruler to make the greatest impact upon mankind. He will boast that with this god at the helm of the planet the invasion can be halted and the world reborn for the good of all mankind. However, with his new found power the Antichrist will be obsessed with his real agenda, stealing the souls of those who haven't accepted the gift of life and destroying those that have. This world dictator will instruct the Minister to construct a demonizing fleet of indestructible humanlike robotic machines to accomplish his agenda. However, the Antichrist must first proceed to the newly constructed Temple in Jerusalem to exercise his newly acquired power and officially declare himself a god. It's gonna get ugly!

ON EAGLE'S WINGS

Satan has sought to seduce and confiscate the souls of mankind since humans first set foot on this earth. He has been especially vindictive of the Israelites because the nation of Israel was the birthplace of Jesus, the long-awaited Messiah of the Jews and the archenemy of Satan. "He made his greatest attempt to destroy the Jewish people under the Third Reich, when Adolf Hitler sent six million Jews to their death."[7]

A surprise attack on Israel will be orchestrated by Satan and led by the Antichrist as retribution for being permanently "kicked out of heaven." However, an early warning system has been devised to alert the Jews who accepted the gift of life that the attack is coming. As mentioned earlier the Antichrist will defile the newly constructed Temple in Jerusalem by entering the Holy area and declaring himself a god. "Jewish believers will recognize this as the sign of the 'abomination of desolation' predicted by Daniel, ... and will flee the city, except for the two witnesses, who remain to oppose the Antichrist and give a worldwide demonstration of God's power."[8]Approximately one-third of the Jews will hear the message of the two prophets, accept the gift of life and escape to the secret hiding place.[9]The manuscripts record Armageddon and the end of the world to be exactly 1,290 days or about three-and-one-half years from the desecration of the Temple. Therefore, this event occurs precisely at the mid-point of the invasion.[10]

A safe haven will be provided for the remainder of the invasion for the Jews who escape. As the Jews flee Israel, Satan will pursue and attack them with everything in his arsenal of supernatural weapons. However, God will intervene and cause the earth to open up and swallow the threat to the Jews. And Satan will lose again!

Israel will be given "two wings of a great eagle" to carry her safely to the secret hiding place.[11] Here, the remnant of the Israelites will be protected until the end of the invasion. One may be tempted to associate the "two wings of a great eagle" with action on the part of the United States, since America has always been a strong ally of the Israelites and our nation is symbolized by an eagle. However, in the ancient manuscripts, it is written that God reminded the Israelites that they were delivered from the bondage of the Egyptians thousands of years ago "on eagle's wings" symbolized by the strength of God.[12] God came to the rescue of the Israelites and He will do it again. Therefore, the expression "two wings of a great eagle" is most likely a symbol of the supernatural deliverance of the Israelites by God, not intervention by the United States, who by this time will likely be powerless to do much of anything.

"… Edom, Moab and Ammon. These ancient countries, which now constitute Jordan, may well be the place God has prepared for the nation of Israel to hide."[13] A possible hiding place in Jordan is Bozrah, the ancient capital of Edom.[14] Another potential place of hiding is the ancient city of Petra which is a natural fortress enclosed on three sides by towering mountains.

The picture illustrates the ancient ruins of the tombs and the amazing Treasury hewn out of the sandstone cliffs by early inhabitants of Edom.

Ruins of the tombs in the ancient city of Petra in Edom, Jordan[15]

The Treasury in the ancient city of Petra in Edom, Jordan[16]

REFLECTIONS

We are now approximately three-and-one-half years into the invasion or about halfway to Armageddon and the end of the world.

- Approximately three-and-one-half years after negotiating a seven-year peace treaty with Israel, the Antichrist will break the treaty.

- Satan will be cast out of heaven to earth for a second time, along with his demonic angels. This time it will be for good.

- The Antichrist will be assassinated and supernaturally resurrected with the spirit and demonic power of Satan.

- The Antichrist will go to the newly constructed Temple in Jerusalem and desecrate the Holy of Holies.

- The abomination of desolation of the Temple will be the signal to the Jews who accepted the gift of life to flee to safety before the attack by the Antichrist and Satan. They will be carried to a secret hiding place to avoid an attack by Satan and his armies near the end of the invasion.

15

THE PIN

*M*ore than thirty years ago our family traveled to Disney World in Florida and visited an exhibit with life-size models of several Presidents of the United States. Sitting behind a long table facing the audience, they looked remarkably real. While we watched, something seemed to activate them and they began a conversation with each other. As each figure spoke, "he" made incredibly life-like gestures while exhibiting realistic body language. Their performance was so convincing, we almost expected them to stand up and walk off. Of course, they didn't. The realism of the figures we experienced was produced with state of the art robotic and electronic technology of thirty years ago. That technology has unquestionably advanced dramatically over the past three decades.

Shortly after the shocking resurrection of the Antichrist, the world will be introduced to the most incredible fleet of walking, talking, human-looking and acting life-size robotic machines ever imagined by mankind. However, these robots will not be developed for the entertainment of curious audiences. The diabolical machines that will infiltrate the world and the message they bear will change the lives of many people forever as they struggle to survive in the last days. Meanwhile the Antichrist will waste no time making his presence known to the world as a "god."

THE "DOOMSDAY MESSAGE"

With the help of his ten world leaders, the Antichrist will destroy the popular ecumenical or global religion (which will be discussed later) that is gaining acceptance as a "fashionable faith" even today. In fact, the only religion that will be embraced by the Antichrist and his government in the last half of the invasion is the worship of himself. The evil dictator will likely even make it illegal to own any religious book and will arrest anyone found to have one in his possession. He will seek to destroy all copies of the collection of ancient manuscripts because they expose his fiendish agenda and provide potential victims the key to the secret of escape from his diabolical clutches. The book once commonplace throughout many parts of the world will find a safe harbor only in the "underground of secrecy" maintained by those who are able to survive under the vigilant radar of the Antichrist and his broad network of supporters.

Meanwhile, the Antichrist will be disheartened by the successful flight of his "prey" from Jerusalem and will be disgusted with the two mystery men who were likely responsible for their escape. Therefore, the Antichrist will have his henchmen blatantly execute the two men in the streets of Jerusalem. The entire world will watch them lie dead in the street for three-and-one-half days. It has only been in recent years that it was possible for the entire world to watch any event live simultaneously due to the development and commercialization of advanced television technology, satellites, computers and the internet.

Much of the world will be so saturated with evil that people will be elated to witness the death of these two men and their troubling "doomsday message" forecasting the end of the world and challenging people to accept the gift of life before it is too late. People will be so happy they will celebrate the event and even exchange gifts.[1] John noticed no one came to help the two men or even attempted to remove their bodies from the street after they were murdered. John probably wanted to help, but he was only an observer. No one could see or hear him since they were separated by centuries of time and space. For more than three days people will just walk around the bodies, refusing to move them out of the street.

> *Of course, this reaction of bystanders to murder or an accident is not all that uncommon today. Although there are heroes, we often see news accounts of accident victims lying in the streets with bystanders just walking by and curiously looking at them. No one calls for help or stops to give aid. People are too busy or too nervous about "getting involved" so they just put blinders on their conscience and go their way.*

Suddenly a voice from above commanded the two men to "come up." To the utter amazement of everyone watching, the two men slowly stood to their feet and shook the dirt off their bodies. Then they ascended to the heavens without uttering a word and vanished from sight while a troubled world watched.[2] Following this startling resurrection, a great earthquake will destroy ten percent of the city of Jerusalem and kill more than seven thousand people as a result of the people's unconcern and vile treatment of the two messengers. And the seventh angel sounded his trumpet.

VALKYRIE OR GESTAPO

The Antichrist will use an evil mark with a secret meaning to identify the victims of the diabolical plan he will unveil during the second half of the invasion. John described the mark of the Antichrist as the number 666.[3] Over the years many have speculated as to the meaning of the number 666 and yet there is no consensus as to what it means. It will always be a secret. However, it is not necessary to understand the meaning of the number, what is much more important is to know why a person living during the invasion must never accept the mark.

Unless it has already happened by the mid-point of the invasion, the Antichrist will complete the conversion of the world's financial infrastructure to a totally electronic cashless system. With this electronic network in place, the push of a button will reveal the location and details of the financial transactions of anyone anywhere in the world at any time. With a global, electronic financial structure coupled to a massive system of computers throughout the world, the Antichrist will be able to monitor and virtually control the lives of every human being on earth who uses the system. However, to control the world everyone must be convinced to use the system. The Antichrist will likely take advantage of the commercial RFID technology discussed earlier to easily and conveniently mark his "victims" with the miniature implant and give them controlled access to the new system. Those who accept the Antichrist's PIN encrypted with the 666, will unknowingly be marked for eternity and seal their destiny in a fate worse than death.

The world leader will empower a company of trained personnel or civilian army to enforce the acceptance of the electronic implants by the population. This group of dedicated personnel will also faithfully seek out, identify and neutralize those who refuse the PIN process and threaten to undermine the Antichrist's plans. Of course, the reasons given for establishing this private army will be to achieve world security objectives, handle any insurrection during the infrastructure reconstruction efforts and control any matters of civil unrest.

How difficult will it be to form a private army in the modern world? Would you be surprised to learn that such a civilian army was proposed by the 44th President of the United States when he was a candidate for office in 2008? The following Associated Press release on November, 11, 2008 recorded this account: "A Republican congressman from Georgia said Monday he fears that President-elect Obama will establish a Gestapo-like security force to impose a Marxist dictatorship. 'It may sound a bit crazy and off base, but the thing is, he's the one who proposed this national security force,' Rep Paul Broun said of Obama in an interview with The Associated Press. 'That's exactly what Hitler did in Nazi Germany and it's exactly what the Soviet Union did,' Broun said. Obama's comments about a national security force came during a speech in Colorado in which he called for expanding the nation's Foreign Service. 'We cannot continue to rely only on our military in order to achieve the national security objectives that we've set,' Obama said in July. 'We've got to have a civilian national security force that's just as powerful, just as strong, just as well-funded.' Broun said he believes Obama would move to ban gun ownership if he does build a national security force."[4]

If the President of the United States can persuade Congress to give him the executive power to create his own personal or private army during peace time, it will be a simple task for the Antichrist to create a dedicated police force in a war-torn world filled with panic, mayhem and turmoil under attack by unknown invaders. Under the dictatorship of Hitler, Germany had a private army called Valkyrie, established to maintain control during any kind of civil unrest. Hitler also had the Gestapo, or secret police which operated with the power to investigate and suppress any activity dangerous to the state. Those who opposed Hitler were arrested or they disappeared! The Antichrist may see the need for his own version of Valkyrie or Gestapo, or both.

The manuscripts don't describe the details of how the Antichrist will actually implement his plan to convince the world's population to embrace his new cashless financial system and accept his PIN. However, with today's technology it's easy to imagine the following scenario.

ROBOTIC MACHINES

The Minister of Propaganda will use the art of deception to convince the CEOs of major companies to fabricate a fleet of robotic clones of the Antichrist with human-like capabilities.[5] He will likely be forced to involve corporations worldwide due to the limited number of companies with the required expertise and fabrication capabilities that have not been destroyed by the invasion. The Minister will use his charismatic personality to deceive the corporate executives and faithfully fulfill the evil agenda of the Antichrist. He will even have the supernatural power to call fire down from the heavens to make his mission more convincing to any who question his request.

The Minister of Propaganda will convince the manufacturers that a realistic-looking clone of the Antichrist will be an admirable expression of gratitude for his contribution to the ongoing restoration of the world and recognition of his god-like powers which will be used for the good of the world. The executives will be honored to participate in this significant venture. The notoriety they receive from the President of the New World Order for their work, as well as a large sum of money to feed their corporate greed, is all that will be necessary to expedite the work. Each life-size robot will be designed to have incredibly realistic physical features identical to the Antichrist.

However, this will be no ordinary robotic figure. The Minister of Propaganda will use his supernatural power to give the completed robot life-like abilities and characteristics.[6]This robotic-clone of the Antichrist will not actually be a living person. However, it will become a supernatural, fully functional robotic machine in the exact image of the Antichrist. It will be capable of most of the functions of a human with convincing facial features, body movements and speech identical to the Antichrist. When energized by the power of Satan, these robots will exhibit capabilities precisely replicating a human the designers never imagined possible. A number of robots will likely be constructed, perhaps thousands of them, and distributed all over the world to infiltrate the population and expedite the work of the Antichrist. In fact, a fleet of robotic machines will be necessary to reach the population of the entire world in the short time remaining.

The role of the robots will be to act as hosts for the Antichrist and persuade people to pledge their allegiance to the resurrected world leader in order to gain access to all the benefits of the new financial system. The real goal of the hosts will simply be to confiscate the soul of every living person with no soul left behind. A special surprise awaits those who refuse to accept the PIN.

"INFORMATION CENTERS"

The Minister of Propaganda, in concert with the media will roll out a well organized marketing strategy to set the Antichrist's diabolical trap. In a television and radio media blitz to the world, the President of the New World Order will explain that the largest industrialized nations of the world have been successful in developing a new totally cashless global electronic currency system. The system has been fully tested and has been operational in industry, business, and government organizations for some time. It is now time to expand the system for use by all individuals. Total implementation of the system by everyone is critical to improving the efficiency and accuracy of all financial transactions, bringing the world closer together, stabilizing the financial markets in the chaos of the worsening invasion, and capitalizing on the dwindling resources in the war torn and disaster ravaged world. The Antichrist will insist that it is imperative to make the transition to the cashless financial system as quickly as possible to accelerate the restoration of order in the world especially in light of the continuing attacks by the invaders.

While the robots are being manufactured, the Minister of Propaganda and his vast organization of supporters will have user-friendly "Information Centers" erected in every major city, town, and strategic location around the world. Everyone will be encouraged by the media to go to the nearest "Information Center" at their earliest convenience. There they will receive additional information about the electronic cashless financial system and the procedure to obtain their

PIN. People will be asked to bring their passports, birth certificates, bank records, investments, medical records and other important documents to expedite their transition to the new paperless financial system. The media will develop a captivating "spin" on the process to encourage immediate participation as directed by the Minister of Propaganda.

The Minister will explain that the world leader would like to speak to each group of people at the "Information Centers" in person but due to the number of centers and time constraints, that will be physically impossible. Therefore, he has arranged to have a life-like representative of himself attend each information session. These clones of the Antichrist will be so life-like people will think he's actually there. The presentations will be much more effective than a conventional video since the clone will be able to interact with the groups on a personal basis and even respond to questions. There will be other members of the staff of the Minister of Propaganda to assist with the work of transferring records and inputting data for those accepting the PIN. Members of the civilian army will also be on hand for crowd control and to handle any difficult issues that might arise.

Once inside the "Information Centers," one of the robotic hosts will answer any questions as he explains how the new cashless currency system will work. The host will then explain that sensitive electronic scanners have already been installed in stores, banks, airports, train stations, grocery and department stores, and other places of business around the world. The host will stress that without the PIN no one will be able to buy or sell goods and services or transact any business of any kind beginning immediately after the offer to participate in the new financial system is extended to them. Cash will not be accepted in any form by anyone. The crowds will be mesmerized by the soft-spoken pleasant but deceptive words of the hosts and overwhelmed by the benefits promised by the new system.

COMPLIMENTARY PIN

Then the host will explain that each person will be able to receive a complimentary electronic identification chip no larger than a grain of rice. The chip will contain a secret encrypted PIN (666) to authenticate the person's identity and password as well as validate his allegiance to the Antichrist when making any financial transaction. Rather than issue a credit card or similar device that could be lost, stolen or counterfeited, the decision was made to utilize a simple implant device that can be painlessly inserted just under the skin of the right hand or forehead, whichever is preferred. The host elaborates with a smile the procedure will only take a few minutes leaving no scar and jokingly remarks you will never leave home without it. The chip has been successfully used in hundreds of cases with no ill-effects and was approved by the United States FDA in 2004 for use in humans in America. He stresses other countries quickly followed the lead of the United States and the chip is now approved for use in humans throughout the world. This chip will enable a person to take advantage of the new electronic cashless financial system immediately. Each of the recipients' financial, personal and medical information will also be included in the PIN, which will simplify many everyday tasks.

At the conclusion of the sales pitch by the host, the group will be led to a separate area where the implants are administered. However, the host explains that prior to receiving the chip each individual must publicly pledge their allegiance to the world leader. He explains that this pledge of allegiance to the President of the New World Order is just a formality. However, it is absolutely necessary to assure that everyone will look to him as the provider of safety and security in this world of chaos and turmoil. Of course, this pledge of commitment will also minimize objectors from undermining the value of the diabolical program. He states the world must be united now more than ever. After all, the New World Order cannot tolerate insurgents who seek to challenge the life promised by the President of the New World Order.

The host explains this is an insignificant request for access to the amazing new financial system that promises to improve the quality of their lives. Most people will see this as a small price to pay for what they believe will be a better life and quickly pledge their allegiance. Swearing loyalty to the new world leader may even be as simple as taking an oath of commitment and pledging their allegiance to the Antichrist and the flag of the New World Order in a public forum. All those who complete the pledge to the world leader will be led to a room where the PIN will be administered. The staff will code and insert the PIN under the skin of each individual. Financial personnel will also be available to transfer the individual's personal and financial records into the new computer system. Once the transfer of a person's records is complete, the host will ask that all cash and checks, be left in a repository located in the "Information Centers." All useless paper will be shredded for security reasons. Those who bear the PIN, the mark of the Antichrist, will be irrevocably condemned to the final destination of the demons and Satan, the eternal land of torment called hell following their death on earth. Those who are uncomfortable with the electronic chip or who choose to refuse the offer for one reason or another will be quietly escorted to another nearby area.

THE GUILLOTINE

The host, with a more somber and almost apologetic tone in his voice, explains there is no way anyone who rejects the PIN can continue to survive since they will not be able to transact business and buy and sell goods. The absence of a PIN will ultimately condemn them to an unavoidable, slow and miserable death as a result of starvation, disease and sickness. The host raises his clenched fist and proclaims the world leader will absolutely not tolerate a black market, theft, or any other means to circumvent the required coded PIN necessary for financial transactions. Therefore, unless they accept the PIN at this time, they will be subjected to a fast, painless method of euthanasia, which is the only humane thing to do.[7] The world leader has only their best interests at heart and desires no one should suffer. At this point, there will probably be a large crowd of people rushing to change their decision. Those who refuse the second opportunity to accept the PIN will be led by the host to another area isolated from the rest of the center and told that they may go home. Anyone believe that? The doors will quietly close and lock and the robotic host will engage his satanic power or call on representatives of the civilian army to restrain those people who will try to escape the fate awaiting them.

In our modern day of technology it is easy to believe the Antichrist will equip the robots with a laser, a neutron gun, poison gas or some other modern weapon to quickly and quietly take the lives of the people in this group. However, people will actually be beheaded for their refusal to worship the Antichrist.[8] The robots will have the power to execute those people by using a device to simply cut off their heads. Now the ancient manuscripts do not give the details of the death machine the Antichrist will use. It is likely he will bring back the infamous guillotine used during the

French Revolution. The guillotine is a proven efficient and fast method of removing one's head, which also provides a very compelling public display to those who have not yet made their final decision.

Two historic replica models of French Guillotines[9]

These devices are simple in design and will be easy to manufacture. Thousands of these death machines can be quickly manufactured and sent to "Information Centers" around the world. The Minister of Propaganda is a master of persuasion, and it will be a simple task to convince companies to build thousands of these devices to deter enemies of the Antichrist from threatening to undermine his power and perhaps plot another assassination. The perpetrators must be brought to justice quickly and others discouraged from participating in such acts of violence. The guillotine machines placed strategically around the world for all to see will be extremely effective in providing a visible deterrent to violence. The word will travel fast!

After extending one last opportunity to everyone to pledge their allegiance to the Antichrist while standing in the shadow of the guillotines, those who still refuse will be made to approach the steps of one of the death machines. As some people come to the stark realization of the consequence of refusing to pledge allegiance to the Antichrist, they will quietly bow in the presence of the machines. They will now accept the gift of life that they have known about for some time but refused to accept for fear of persecution by the Antichrist.

So ends the earthly lives of those who refuse the offer of the Antichrist. They will die as martyrs and take their place in eternity with God. As the executions continue, many in the room will decide that taking the PIN of the Antichrist is not a bad alternative to losing their head and beg the host to retreat back to the area where they can obtain their PIN. Many will trade eternity in heaven for a mere three-and-one-half more years or less of dreadful existence on earth and a destination in eternity worse than death. As the word of the executions spread, many people throughout the world will go into hiding rather than go to one of the "Information Centers." Although the civilian army of the Antichrist will seek out and execute those who flee the PIN process, countless thousands will escape and accept the gift of life.

REFLECTIONS

- The Antichrist will have the two messengers of the gift of life murdered in the streets of Jerusalem.

- The two men will be supernaturally, miraculously resurrected after three-and-one-half days.

- An earthquake will destroy ten percent of the city of Jerusalem and kill more than 7,000 people as judgment for the people and their vile treatment of the two messengers.

- Life-like supernatural clones of the Antichrist will be manufactured and sent out to infiltrate the earth. They will seduce the population into joining the forces of the Antichrist and accept his PIN (666) with the promise of a better life.

- Many will receive the implanted electronic PIN with the encrypted code of the Antichrist and seal their fate in eternity.

- Many will die at the hands of the robotic hosts as martyrs for accepting the gift of life and refusing to pledge allegiance to the Antichrist.

16

TALE OF TWO CITIES

*a*s the invasion proceeds beyond the halfway mark, John is distracted from the death, mayhem and devastation of mankind. Suddenly he focuses on the appealing image of a mysteriously beautiful woman with a wild and seductive appearance as she languishes in the spotlight of worldly notoriety. She is not a diplomat, a popular movie actress or even a rock star, but she is known and loved by heads of state throughout the world as well as the general population. Who is this woman and why is it critical to understand her motive and the role she plays in the lives of mankind today and in the future? Learn why this fashionable personality with an insatiable passion for people will be destroyed by the Antichrist as the catastrophic effects of the invasion continue to mount. However, before we are introduced to this mystery woman, John will witness the impact of five more devastating attacks on the planet.

John saw seven angels each holding a supernatural vial filled with suffering and torment. They stood patiently ready to unleash the last seven stages of mass destruction by emptying the contents of each of their vials onto the earth. Imagine the terror permeating the population as the first vial was poured out on the earth launching the third and last offensive of the invasion.

THE THIRD OFFENSIVE

DEADLY DECISION

John heard a voice which gave the first angel the signal to step up and release the contents of his vial targeting only people who accepted the PIN. The angel was not allowed to cause anyone to suffer who denounced the Antichrist and accepted the gift of life. The contents of the vial will blanket the earth like a cloud and immediately, those identified with the PIN will be infected with a body rotting plague that will cause the flesh to erupt in horrible festering sores.[1] The victims will wrench in unbelievable pain and scream for relief but the call for help will be in vain. Those who pledged their allegiance to the Antichrist will immediately begin to pay the price; they made the wrong deadly decision and there is no turning back. The world's leaders will likely blame this horrific outbreak on a mysterious highly contagious mutated strain of disease that was broadcast over the earth by the invaders using some futuristic weapon of mass destruction. The fact that the disease seemed to infect only those with the PIN implant will baffle the doctors. Of course some people may be suspicious that the implants are contaminated.

A VICIOUS VIRUS

The second angel emptied his vial into the seas and as the contents spread like a vicious virus throughout the oceans every living thing in the seas died and the water turned to blood.[2] One-third of the oceans turned to blood due to an earlier attack; now all the water in the oceans and seas will turn to blood leaving no sea life of any kind alive. This annihilation of sea creatures will greatly compound the spiraling food shortage brought about by the earlier assaults. In addition, the air above the oceans that eventually drifts to the mainland will be polluted with the unimaginable stench of vast seas of decaying blood mixed with rotting carcasses of people and marine life. Also, the thousands of desalinization plants, critical for the conversion of sea water to fresh water on ships, islands and coastlines around the world, will be poisoned by the blood and debris and quickly rendered inoperative. An important source of fresh water necessary to sustain life will be eliminated. With most of the population experiencing the body rotting plague resulting from the previous attack, the impact of this virus will send the world reeling. Scientists will question how the invaders successfully injected another superhuman biological weapon of mass destruction into the oceans and destroyed a vital source of food and impacted the fresh water supply.

THE PROMISE OF DEATH

John saw the third angel pour out his vial filled with the promise of death on all the rivers, streams and spring fed tributaries of the earth.[3] The water polluted with blood will quickly be carried into the lakes, reservoirs and water treatment plants of cities and municipalities throughout the world eliminating the major sources of drinking water on the planet. Blood will gush from all the water faucets, fountains and lawn sprinklers. Fireman will be stunned to see blood rather than water spraying onto burning structures from their fire hoses. People will be terrified by the never ending sight of blood and the shocking shortage of fresh water. Mankind will be left with only the available supply of bottled water and any water that can be collected from rainfall. Water may be available from underground aquifers if they are not already contaminated by the contents of the third vial.

There will be an immediate insatiable demand for water because mankind cannot live more than a few days without the miracle liquid. In fact, water, once the most plentiful liquid on earth will quickly become the liquid gold of the twenty-first century, hotly pursued by all who struggle to live. Many people will die fighting for possession of a few bottles of water, a victory that will simply prolong the futile battle for life. To further complicate the fight to survive, the polluted water will render most, if not all, the waste treatment facilities in the world inoperative. Soon the world will be drowning in mankind's own growing mountain of waste. Finally, the wildlife that depends on water to live will soon die and eliminate one more of the important sources of food for the human race. It will seem that the deadly biological weapon of mass destruction from space was successfully introduced again into the planet's bodies of water undetected by mankind. Scientists will diligently analyze the contaminated water searching for clues to the identity of the virus and a way to reverse the impact of the unknown biological weapon but their work will be in vain. People will be screaming in the streets "what else can happen to us?" If they only knew what was yet to come.

PRESCRIPTION FOR HORROR

While mankind grappled with the pain of sores on their bodies and the search for fresh water, the fourth angel emptied his vial containing a prescription for horror that will burn the bodies of mankind and exacerbate their misery due to the lack of precious drinking water.[4] This affliction may take place due to a supernatural increase in the temperature of the sun, which is already a scorching 10,000 degrees F. The searing burns may be caused by simply increasing the amount of ultraviolet light reaching the earth's surface. Scientists today are concerned about a thinning of the protective ozone layer in the upper atmosphere which limits the amount of ultraviolet light reaching the earth. The end result is that the skin of mankind will be subjected to painful, sunburn for which there will be absolutely no relief.

Severe sunburn is miserable and this sunburn will be so horrible that people will angrily curse God out of desperation. People will fight and be willing to die for any small parcel of cover to shade them from the scorching rays of the sun. The weather reports around the world will forecast cloudless skies with no rain ever in sight. Crops will die due to the heat and drought, contributing to the nearly exhausted food supply. People will die by the thousands from heat exhaustion and increasing lack of water. All work outside will be suspended. Electricity shortages will be rampant throughout the world since many electrical generating plants will be shut down due to a lack of cooling water. Scientists and astronomers will be bewildered by how the invaders are able to mysteriously increase the amount of ultraviolet light reaching the earth's surface. The intruders must be from a highly developed civilization with powers far beyond those of humans on earth.

CANOPY OF DARKNESS

While the rest of the world suffered from the blistering heat of the sun, the fifth angel poured out the contents of his vial directly over the city where the world headquarters of the Antichrist is located.[5] A mysterious canopy of total darkness descended over the entire city plunging the population into the darkest of night. People will panic in the dark and be unable to function. It's likely there will be

203

no lights due to the electrical generating stations being shut down. Traffic will be snarled and tempers flaring. The effect of the scorching sun will be gone but the anguish of the painful sunburn and excruciating sores will remain. People will gnaw their tongues from the unbearable pain inflicted by the previous attacks and curse God in the darkness. Astronomers will strain through their telescopes looking for some mammoth device in space between the earth and the sun that could be casting such a shadow over the city. There will be no such device discovered.

> *Have you ever been in a cave deep underground when the guide tells you to hold on to something or someone because the lights are going to go out? Remember you couldn't see your hand in front of your face. That's dark. My wife and I were exposed to this kind of darkness in a solitary confinement cell during a tour of Alcatraz. We were in the dark cell for only a minute or two and we were more than ready to open the door and get out into the light. There is something terrifying about absolute total darkness! Add excruciating pain from sunburn to the horror of total darkness and you have a recipe for terror.*

There is a brief intermission before the next two angels empty the final two vials of misery and destruction. During this time John is finally introduced to that mysterious and incredible looking image of the woman he saw. Although this next event is bizarre to say the least, it's important to

204

understand the impact of this woman on the generation living today. You may even recognize her.

THE BEAUTY AND THE BEAST

The Image

One of the angels responsible for releasing the contents of the seven vials of terror pointed to the image of the mysterious woman and graphically described her to John as the "great whore that sits upon many waters."[6] I'm sure John was a little taken back by the language used by the angel but he was awestruck by the image of a seductive-looking, beautiful woman sitting on the back of an unusual, scarlet colored animal. The woman had a wild look about her and the strange beast had seven heads and ten horns. What a startling picture of the beauty and the beast but this image is not out of the movie you may be familiar with. John had never seen anything like it. What does the image represent and why is it important for us to understand the meaning of this bizarre encounter today?

The angel explained to John that this woman committed fornication with the leaders of the great nations of the world and made the population of the earth drunk with the wine of that fornication. Therefore, we quickly realize as did John, this is not the image of a real woman. It makes no sense. No woman could have sex with all the heads of state and leaders of nations in the world. Since a literal interpretation makes absolutely no sense, we must search for additional meaning. The significance of this image spans centuries of time and will climax during the future invasion of earth. This is obviously a case where a vivid illustration or image was used to help John grasp an important but complex subject. After all, a picture is worth a thousand words. You see examples of this technique used in television commercials every day. A slick marketing campaign uses simple images, illustrations or even cartoons to make a very complicated issue easy for the viewer to understand. Fortunately, the angel will explain the mystery of the bizarre image.

The Beauty

As John looked closer he saw that the woman in the image was lavishly adorned in expensive garments of purple and scarlet, colors usually representative of kings and queens. She was "dressed to kill" with gold, pearls and precious stones to dazzle, charm and lure her prey. Her wickedness and evil agenda was cleverly concealed by her alluring, seductive beauty. She was holding a golden cup and John believed she was intoxicated because he saw something that looked like red wine spilling from the cup. The angel explained there is blood in the cup and that the woman was drunk with the blood of those who accepted the gift of life. John was probably nauseated at the sight because it reminded him of the persecution and deaths of so many of his friends by the brutal Roman Empire. You see, John belonged to the "Chosen" and possessed the gift of life. The angel could tell by the bewildered look of wonder on John's face that he didn't yet fully comprehend the meaning of the mysterious imagery that he was witnessing. How could he possibly record this mystery when he still didn't understand the meaning of the woman?

What does it mean that this woman committed fornication with the kings of the earth and all the inhabitants, and if she is not a woman, what is she? In the ancient manuscripts "… the terms 'whore', 'harlot', and 'adulterer' are frequently used to symbolize a spiritual departure from God and His truth by an individual, a city or a nation. The word 'harlot' is especially used to describe a religion that is counterfeit."[7]

TALE OF TWO CITIES

For example, thousands of years ago God accused Israel of playing the harlot and committing whoredom with idols made of wood and stone.[8] In other words, the Israelites were forsaking the fundamental worship of God and giving their allegiance to a counterfeit religion.

Therefore, this woman is simply an allegorical representation of a false religion, a counterfeit or idol-worshipping faith. The act of adultery is the seduction of people by the woman (organized false religion) to participate in the worship of idols. It's a well-known fact that false religions with appealing beliefs and lucrative promises will lure people to their folds much like a flame attracts moths. This is very true today. Of course, the ultimate destiny of the moth is death from the flame.

> *Granted, you probably don't know anyone who worships a wood or stone object. However, haven't you known those who almost worshipped movie stars, rock stars or sports figures? What about people who are so engaged in activities of leisure that they put the pursuit of pleasure ahead of everything else in life, regardless of the cost? Any endeavor we become obsessed with is dangerous to our livelihood. We'll see that a religious system created by mankind that appeals to our sense of self-gratification and makes promises without substance to fill a spiritual vacuum will ultimately prove to be deadly.*

The angel explained that this woman and what she stands for is exceedingly popular with people throughout the world. "This can only mean a one-world religious system."[9] Therefore, the angel is trying to explain that a global counterfeit religion, rooted in idolatry and the pleasures of the world will spread like wildfire throughout the world just prior to the invasion. The people ensnared in this fashionable religion will be lured away from every traditional religious denomination as well as those people who claim no religion.

> We must be ever vigilant of the progress of the ecumenical or one-world religion and its infiltration into congregations of traditional churches in our day as it gains momentum. Like the seductive woman in the image, the popular false religion will attract and mesmerize people by offering them pleasure, entertainment and all forms of self-gratification. It will also offer unsuspecting worshippers the empty promises of a more prosperous life, good health and pleasure with a clear path to heaven. This trendy, fashionable religion will broadcast a spiritual call for global unity, an amalgamation of the world's religions and the general acceptance of compromise in order to avoid offending any religious faith.

People will commit fornication with this woman or counterfeit religion today and in the future by blindly subscribing to the beliefs and participating in the practices of that religion. Satisfied with the routine "feel-good messages" of a stylish religion, people will abandon or perhaps never begin the search for the secrets to the real treasures of life. There will be no interest in discovering the secret to surviving the end of the world because they won't embrace the reality of the warning that the world will end! It will not be until after the invasion has begun that many will realize they were defrauded by the enticing vogue message of the counterfeit religion. After a brief look at the identity of the animal the woman is riding, we'll examine the connection between the woman responsible for the blood of those who opposed her and the city of Rome, believed by many to be the future home of the great harlot and the headquarters of the Antichrist.

The Beast

After explaining the meaning of the woman to John, the angel sought to make clear the relationship between the woman (the one-world religion) and the beast (Antichrist) during the invasion. The beast John saw had seven heads and ten horns. The angel pointed out that the seven heads of the beast are seven mountains and there are seven kings or world empires. We're not told who the seven kings are or what empires they represent. We do know that five of the most powerful empires of the world had disappeared by John's time (Egypt, Assyria, Babylon, Persia and Greece) and the sixth, Rome, was in power at that time. We also know that Domitian was the Roman Emperor at the time John was living. Finally, it's generally accepted that the Antichrist, or the beast, is the seventh king or head of the world empire of the future.

Then the angel gave John a strange riddle explaining the recent transformation of the Antichrist (the beast). "And the beast that was, and is not, even he is the eighth and is of the seven..."[10] John must have understood the riddle since he didn't ask for further explanation. "Probably the seventh ruler is the Beast in his human form, the form he assumes when he first appears as the beast out of the sea and the eighth ruler is the Beast in his superhuman form, the form he assumes when he reappears after his assassination, as the Beast out of the abyss."[11] So the seventh and eighth ruler in what appears to be a confusing riddle is simply the Antichrist. He initially emerged from the population of people descending from the ancient Roman Empire (the sea of people) to world politics. Following his death he emerged to life from the bottomless pit (the abyss) by the power of Satan.

The angel explained that the ten horns John saw are ten kings or heads of nations that will receive power from the Antichrist. This seems to be a clear reference to the evolving federation of nations (European Union) that have recently emerged from the ruins of the ancient Roman Empire as described by Daniel.

The City

Rome has often been referred to as the "city of seven hills." This is our first clue that the city of Rome may play a significant role in understanding this strange image. The angel explained to John that the woman he saw is that great city which reigns over the kings of the earth. However, a city doesn't reign over anyone. We know it's the Antichrist who reigns over the earth during the invasion. What does the angel mean? We can only speculate that the evil work of the religious atrocity disguised as a woman is threaded throughout the fabric of the history of ancient Rome and that perhaps modern Rome will be the world headquarters of the Antichrist. "In the last days Rome, as a religious system is clearly linked with Babylon and Babylon with Rome."[12]

Then John noticed the words "Mystery, Babylon the Great, the Mother of Harlots and Abominations of the Earth" on the woman's forehead. It's as though she was indelibly stenciled or tattooed to warn her unsuspecting victims of her true identity. However, as she sweeps her prey off their feet with her fatal attraction and enticing promises, probably no one would even notice the warning.

> *The angel is warning us to look closely at the appeal of religious organizations and determine if they provide fundamental spiritual value or just offer the empty promises of a compromising message designed to accommodate everyone without offending anyone!*

The reference to the city of Babylon on the forehead of the woman must give us another clue to the city she possesses. The site of the ancient tower of Babel eventually became the location for the sin city of Babylon built by Nebuchadnezzar on the banks of the Euphrates River. Think of Babylon as a code word in the manuscripts saying one thing but meaning something completely different. When people anywhere in the world hear the word Wall Street, most people do not think of a crowded, narrow street in the financial district of lower Manhattan, New York City. They would identify Wall Street with the New York Stock Exchange, the American Stock Exchange and the NASDQ Stock Exchange. It would bring to mind the headquarters for investments in stocks, bonds, commodities, options, and the massive "golden bull" in the financial district that represents the hope of investors for a prosperous "bull market." Similarly, Babylon doesn't just communicate the name of an ancient city on the banks of the Euphrates River, but rather the birthplace of idolatry and false religion that is still alive and well today throughout the world. "The city of Babylon continued to be the seat of Satan until the fall of the Babylonian and Medo-Persian Empires, when he shifted his capital to Pergamos in Asia Minor, where it was in John's day. When Attatus, the Pontiff and King of Pergamos, died in B.C. 133, he bequeathed the Headship of the 'Babylonian Priesthood' to Rome."[13] "Mystery Babylon! The system has survived the centuries, and it lives on in many a pagan religion in the world today and reigns supreme in Rome. Rome is certainly not the *mother* of harlots and abominations, for that title belongs to ancient Babylon-but she certainly is included. The intoxicating wine of idolatry with all its accompanying vileness was already bottled and labeled three thousand years before Rome was dreamed of; but Rome is a major purveyor of this merchandise."[14]

The golden bull in the financial District, New York City, New York
Photograph by J.E. Bouvier

So Rome was not the cradle for the birth of false religion and idolatry. However, Rome does get credit for the spilling of blood of countless thousands of men and women by burning them at the stake, hanging them on Roman crosses and offering them as food to hungry lions purely for the entertainment of the Emperor and the Roman citizens.

"Whenever in control of a country Rome has not hesitated to put to death all who oppose her."[15]

The End

The angel explained that the ten horns (the New World Order) will hate the whore and ultimately destroy the religious system.[16] "The kings of the earth hate the woman because she represents a threat to their own power. She wields an authority that they feel rightly belongs to them. It was one thing for them to court the whore and to use the Babylonian religious system to expedite the unification of the empire. To tolerate her and her political meddling once the end has been achieved is another matter. The religious system soon becomes an unwanted encumbrance, and the Beast himself has other ideas about the kind of religion suitable for mankind."[17]

The fact that the harlot is riding the beast indicates that she will have tremendous influence on the political system of the Antichrist until about the mid-point of the invasion. The Antichrist will tolerate the false religion or one-world church until he emerges with his supernatural demonic power following his resurrection. Then he will put his own religion in place, the worship of himself as a god. "Antichrist will permit the one-world church to govern his actions during the first three-and-a-half years … while he is gathering more and more power;…when he feels he can become an autocratic ruler, he and the ten kings will throw off the harlot because, in reality, while being dominated by her they 'hate the harlot…' When it is no longer necessary, the ten kings will 'make her desolate and naked, and shall eat her flesh, and burn her with fire' meaning they will confiscate her temples, her gold, and her costly apparel."[18] This will be the end of the harlot and the one-world religious system.

Even today the trendy one-world religion or ecumenical religious system will lure its unsuspecting prey into a false sense of security and complete spiritual complacency while precluding the victims from discovering the true secret to surviving the end of the world. As the beginning of the end draws near, countless millions of defrauded church members will be left to suffer through the terrifying cataclysmic invasion of earth. Soon the spiritually wounded will find themselves the target of the diabolical dictator whose only agenda will be to seize their soul for all eternity. Be very cautious about whose religious beliefs you embrace!

After the destruction of the ecumenical one-world religion, three of the ten kings or leaders of nations in the New World Order will challenge the agenda of the resurrected Antichrist. That challenge will be met in a heartbeat when the Antichrist will brutally destroy the three leaders.[19]After this example of cruel and swift vengeance the world dictator will arrogantly reign over the world for the last few years of the invasion without opposition and without a competing religious system.

REFLECTIONS

- The first vial of destruction will bring painful sores and boils to those who accept the PIN of the Antichrist.

- The devastation produced by the second vial will turn the oceans and seas to blood, killing all forms of sea life.

- The wrath of the third vial will turn the rivers and streams to blood, eliminating almost every source of drinking water.

- The fury unleashed by the fourth vial will result in the sun scorching the skin of mankind with no possible relief.

- The power released by the fifth vial will plunge the headquarters of the Antichrist and the city where it's located into total darkness.

- John was introduced to the strange image of a mysterious woman and the beast. The woman is actually the symbol of the ecumenical global religion of idolatry or one-world religion of compromising faith-a counterfeit religion.

- The Antichrist and his government will tolerate the ecumenical religion or one-world church until about the middle of the invasion when he will destroy the religion and set himself up as a god of his own religion.

- Three of the leaders of the ten nations in the Antichrist's government will rebel against him only to be quickly destroyed.

17
DEATH VALLEY

---

*a*s the "Doomsday Clock" ticks off the final months of the seven-year invasion of earth, there will only be two vials of destruction remaining to be disbursed. Knowing that the end is near, the Commander-in-Chief of the global earthly armies, the Antichrist, will prepare for a final "showdown" with the invaders responsible for the devastation of earth. If the invasion continues, the fractured infrastructures of the earth necessary for humanity's survival will collapse like a "house of cards." Meanwhile, John's attention turned to one of the greatest modern cities in the world where the headquarters of the Antichrist is located. This city is in the crosshairs of an unimaginable weapon of mass destruction contained in the sixth supernatural vial. Discover the identity of this great city and learn why it will be targeted for annihilation. It will literally be "wiped off the face of the earth" in a matter of minutes.

DESTINATION-THE MIDDLE EAST

THE LAST MONTHS

The Antichrist's last act of seduction will be to utilize the powers of darkness to convince the leaders of the world's armies to rally about him in launching a united global assault against the invaders. The overwhelming desperation of the world's leaders to strike back at those responsible for the destruction of earth will surprisingly coincide with the invitation from the powerful Antichrist to stage a massive assault against the invaders. If the military leaders join the Antichrist and are successful, they will free the world from future attacks. However, this agreement will be a commitment to a valiant suicide mission with absolutely no hope of success. This battle will be a war of the worlds that even H.G. Wells could not have imagined. Some of the military commanders may require a little encouragement to agree to immediately move their troops and war machines from ongoing battles around the world and prepare to go against the power of the unknown invaders. Just then John saw a bizarre manifestation of demonic creatures emerging out of the bodies of the Antichrist, the Minister of Propaganda and the ghostly appearance of Satan.[1]

John noticed that each of the three demons appeared as an apparition in the supernatural form of a frog. Imagine that each demon emerged as a mystical translucent vapor with long tentacles like frog's legs floating nervously, anxious to move on with their devilish mission. What a sight! These diabolical ghostly life-forms may ultimately take the form of humans disguised as devoted political supporters of the Antichrist with access to all the modern tools of communication to expedite their mission. Or they may be more subtle and just work their evil as supernatural demonic spirits sowing the seeds of the Antichrist's strategies in the fertile minds of the world's leaders. Time is running out for the Antichrist! With the added pressure from the dictator, the diabolical demons will easily convince the military leaders to gather their personnel, war machines and weapons of mass destruction and deliver them to a predetermined destination in the Middle East as soon as possible. The plan is coming together.

THE STAGING GROUND FOR ARMAGEDDON

John saw the Antichrist gathering the armies of the world together in a place called Armageddon where they will prepare for what John called the "battle of that great day of God Almighty," the war that will end the existence of humanity.[2] Armageddon is the Hebrew name for a hill in modern-day Israel known as Mount Megiddo. This hill overlooking the Valley of Jezreel is north of Jerusalem and a short distance east of the modern seaport city of Haifa on the shores of the Mediterranean Sea. This valley has long since been known for many famous battles throughout history and could be called the "death valley" of the Middle East. "Many leaders have fought battles here, including Napoleon, who said, 'This is the world's greatest natural battlefield.' Other leaders who have fought here include Titus, Pompey, Richard the Lionhearted, Nebuchadnezzar and Rameses. The Mount of Megiddo is soaked and drenched with blood. Why? Because it was an ancient crossroads where trade caravans traveled back and forth. Whoever controlled Megiddo controlled the land, the trade, and the commerce of that day."[3] Maps of the terrain of the valley indicate it's a flat plain, perfect for staging massive numbers of military personnel, equipment and war machines. Ironically, the Antichrist has chosen this war worn valley of Jezreel to be the perfect "gathering place" for his global armies.

The battle of Armageddon will take place only in the Middle East in several nearby locations. The battle in Edom, which was mentioned earlier as a probable hiding place for the remnant of the Jews will signal the beginning of Armageddon.[4] The valley of Jezreel at Mount Megiddo will be the perfect location for what will be a horrific bloodbath for the worldwide armies in another battle. The ancient manuscripts indicate the valley of Jehoshaphat will also be the perfect site for a deadly battle.[5] This area is thought to be part of the Kidron Valley lying between the Temple Mount and the Mount of Olives. The location of the final bloody battle is the city of Jerusalem.[6] Of course, some or all of the battles could take place simultaneously.

A RIVER RUNS DRY

The armies of the world will arrive by air, sea and land in the valley of Jezreel, the staging ground for the approaching war. The only impediment to the approach of massive ground troops from the east will be the Euphrates River which begins its journey in the mountains of Armenia. It flows southwesterly across Turkey, then south through Syria and Iraq by the banks of what was once the ancient city of Babylon and ends in the Persian Gulf.

When the sixth angel released his vial of supernatural power, the flow of water to the great River Euphrates was completely shut off.[7] Once the flow of water stops the riverbed will dry out, allowing the ground troops of the nations to the east to cross easily and make their way to the valley of Jezreel. Of course, today aircraft can provide massive airlifts for troops and equipment and there are bridges over the Euphrates River for land traffic. However, with the wars in the Middle East during the invasion, the bridges will likely have been destroyed. The flow of water for this great river will be shut off, but how will it happen?

In 1990, history was made by the completion of the construction of the mammoth Ataturk Dam on the Euphrates River in Turkey. The flow of the river was all but stopped for a period of time in order to fill the reservoir behind the dam. Therefore, with this marvel of modern-day construction and the chain of dams behind it, the flow of water to the Euphrates River can easily be shut off. Perhaps when the supernatural power of the sixth vial is released the huge gates in the Ataturk dam will mysteriously begin to close until the water stops flowing. In the intense desert heat it won't take long for the riverbed to simply "dry up."

Meanwhile, the troops will pour into the Valley of Jezreel below Mount Megiddo from all over the world. The Mediterranean Sea, the Persian Gulf and nearby seaports like Haifa will be crowded with warships filled to capacity with troops, supplies and weapons. The skies will be darkened with squadrons of aircraft whose destinations will be the makeshift airfields in the Jezreel Valley. Massive numbers of military troops, communications equipment, and war machines will be staged and readied for deployment to the valley.

While the armies of the world proceeded to the staging ground in the Middle East, John was distracted by a phenomenal inferno in the city where the headquarters of the Antichrist was located.

"THAT GREAT CITY"

THE LAST WEEKS

John witnessed the total annihilation of a future commercial and financial icon that will be known for international banking, finance, commerce and global government. In fact, John referred to this metropolis as "that great city" four different times emphasizing its significance in the world.[8] This great capital will be the center of the world's wealth and prosperity as well as the epicenter of evil. The city will also be the world headquarters for the Antichrist and the New World Order where he will orchestrate his unprecedented and brutal rule of the earth. An angel informed John that this city must be destroyed now because she has ruthlessly murdered so many of the "Chosen" in past centuries. It's the only justice.

Many believe this world metropolis destined for destruction is the rebuilt city of Babylon on the banks of the Euphrates River. Saddam Hussein spent more than a billion dollars rebuilding part of the ancient city of Babylon as a monument to himself before his capture and execution in 2006. He completed several buildings of the original city including a monstrous lavishly furnished palace for himself next to the ruins of Nebuchadnezzar's palace on the banks of the Euphrates River. He even scribed his name on many of the bricks imitating the original builder and king of the ancient city. However, there is no evidence that anyone ever occupied the palace. There is no question that a portion of the city of Babylon has been magnificently rebuilt and exists today. There is also no denying the many predictions in the ancient manuscripts that demand the rebuilding of the ancient city of sin. However, the empty unfinished city is far from being able to boast of having the financial and commercial significance of "that great city" described in the ancient manuscripts. Can this reconstructed "ghost city of the past" develop into a world-renowned center of finance and commerce and emerge someday as "that great city?"

Others believe "that great city" is the modern city of Rome, Italy, the same city that may serve as the epicenter of the counterfeit or one-world religion represented by the mysterious "woman." On a recent visit to Rome, my wife and I were fascinated by the well-preserved condition of the blood-stained ruins of structures of the once powerful Roman Empire like the infamous Coliseum. Even more impressive is the remains of the actual throne in the Coliseum where the formidable emperors of Rome sat during the deadly games organized for their pleasure and the entertainment of the Roman citizens. Standing in close proximity to the throne, we were reminded of the god-like powers an emperor exhibited during the games when he could permit a defeated gladiator to live or die with a simple gesture of his hand. It's blood from brutal rulers like these self-proclaimed gods of the ancient Roman Empire that will course through the veins of the diabolical dictator, the Antichrist.

The magnificent Coliseum in Rome, Italy
Photograph by J.E. Bouvier

We were also astounded by the incredible wealth of the Vatican, the epicenter of Catholicism and a country in its own right within the city limits of Rome. The Rome of today is a modern center of transportation and an international crossroads for air, land and rail traffic. Civitavecchia is a modern seaport providing Rome with a gateway to the world of business and commerce. While the economy is somewhat dependent on tourism, it's also a major center for banking, finance and fashion design in its own right. This city with an urban population of more than three million people in 2007 shares the ruins of impressive ancient history of the powerful Roman Empire with modern world prominence. It's truly a magnificent city today.

Hal Lindsey said of "that great city" described by John, "This city can only be Rome. How could Rome not be the capital of the Revived Roman Empire? That this great city is called "Babylon" is no surprise either. It's synonymous with all the evil, corruption, dissoluteness, sensuality and perversion of ancient Babylon and its reprobate child, religion."[9]

We read earlier that the seven heads of the beast on which the "woman" sits are seven mountains. Rome is known geographically for being located on seven hills. On a recent visit to Rome, I noticed the seven mountains or more appropriately, the Seven Hills of Rome were easily identified from our vantage point high above the city. However, the Seven Hills of Rome were probably much more prominent and looked more like seven mountains in John's day as he described them than they are today. The erosion of the mountains over the last two thousand years has been filling in the valleys and has literally transformed the mountains into hills of increasingly smaller dimensions.

John saw the captains and crews of the ships involved with commerce of the great city watching the blaze and smoke rising out of the city from their vessels safely anchored out in the sea.[10] They cried as this world icon of banking, finance, commerce and wealth was decimated since this will be the "nail in the coffin" for the world's financial infrastructure. The modern city of Rome is approximately 90 miles from the port of Civitavecchia on the Mediterranean Sea. Granted, you cannot see Rome from the port because the hills near the ocean obstruct the view. However, as our cruise ship left the port, I could easily imagine seeing the distant skies over the city of Rome brightly lit with the flames of destruction. The ships and the crews on board in the Mediterranean Sea will have no problem witnessing the destruction of Rome firsthand. Babylon on the other hand, is more than 300 miles from the Persian Gulf, the waterway for commerce to reach the shipping lanes in the Mediterranean Sea.

Finally, the angel explained that the city that will be destroyed was responsible for the blood of the prophets and the saints. The Roman Empire, which had its headquarters and the palace of the emperor in Rome, was known for relentlessly and unmercifully persecuting, torturing and killing tens of thousands of people including Christians who challenged the emperor worship of the Roman government.

WARNING

The destruction of "that great city" will likely occur sometime in the last days of the invasion prior to Armageddon. According to the ancient manuscripts this is the only city in the world that will be specifically targeted for destruction during the invasion. In fact, this will actually be the second time that this city will be directly in the crosshairs of a weapon used in the invasion. However, before destruction is delivered to "that great city" a warning is given for anyone in the city who has accepted the gift of life to leave immediately; otherwise, they will be destroyed. The destruction will be so swift that once it strikes, there will be no time to escape. Isn't it interesting that in the midst of imminent destruction, God still seeks to provide refuge for those who possess the gift of life?

The manuscripts do not provide the details about how the city will be destroyed although they clearly indicate it will be decimated by fire in only an hour.[11] Imagine a major city with a population of more than three million people stretching for miles in every direction being totally destroyed in sixty minutes. To obliterate a city that size in one hour would take several nuclear warheads or perhaps one gigantic asteroid barreling down onto the great city from outer space.

THE LAST STATE OF THE WORLD ADDRESS

In January of each year, the President of the United States makes a nationally televised "State of the Union Address" to all Americans. The purpose of this address is for the President to explain his perspective of the present condition of the nation, describe the opportunities and challenges for the coming year, and discuss the plans for Congress and the American people to deal with those opportunities and challenges. The Antichrist will likely present a similar "State of the World Address" when he assumes the office of President of the New World Order and ruler of the world.

The Antichrist will make the initial address to the world just to hear his own rhetoric resonate to the crowds. He will capture the attention of the population with his charismatic style, imagination and creative ideas. He will "explain away" the strange disappearance of people and deliver strategies to calm the chaos in the world. This arrogant, egotistical ruler will likely manufacture scores of empty promises while taking on the aura, popularity and affection of a modern-day rock star attracting enormous crowds wherever he goes. People will be lured into believing everything he says and shower him with accolades.

However, imagine that the last state of the world address may sound something like the following.

"More than seven years ago you chose me by unanimous popular vote to lead the world out of uncontrolled chaos caused by the unexplained disappearance of hundreds of millions of people throughout the world, and I have delivered on my promises. I designed and implemented a new world government that could deal more effectively with the restoration of the fractured infrastructures of the planet. I demanded the scientific community quickly determine the identity of the perpetrators and seek ways to prevent further attacks. I instituted a revolutionary global financial system that repaired the disheveled markets, provided unparalleled security from further failure and gave those who participated in the system a guarantee of a better life while living in the shadow of hopelessness. Despite many accusations against me and my administration, I categorically deny the charge that the PIN system was a covert attempt to gain control of the world. It was absolutely necessary for the human race to survive. There is also no truth to the claim that those who refused to participate in the system are missing. By their own choice they refused the benefits of my lifesaving program and therefore I cannot be held responsible for their welfare.

I regret that we have been unable to stop the incessant attacks from invaders we believe to be from another world with weapons superior to our own. Somehow, they have been able to turn the forces of nature of our own world against us and redirect cosmic bodies in space to target our cities and towns. The invaders have poisoned our water supplies, destroyed our sources of food and dispersed biological weapons that attacked our bodies. They have even infected the minds of the leaders of nations, causing them to recklessly launch recently acquired nuclear weapons in pre-emptive strikes against other nations as far away as the United States. As a result I have been unable to arrest the cause of wars that progressed to an epidemic proportion. Although we don't know the exact origin of these invaders or their mission, the ghastly looking creatures have been sighted around the world as they attacked, tortured and killed innocent victims. From their description they are definitely not of this world!

Recently my headquarters was completely destroyed by the invaders. Fortunately, I was in a remote location with my cabinet members and leaders of all the great military forces planning a massive global offensive against the invaders. I have obtained information that the mastermind of the invasion will soon appear on the earth at a known location in the Middle East. Therefore, the armed forces of the world have pledged their support to mount what will be an all-out-attack against the leader of the invaders when he arrives. I am the President of the New World Order and I expect to be victorious in this great battle. We will soon begin rebuilding our shattered world. You can take that to the bank."

REFLECTIONS

- Three strange demons will convince the military leaders of all the great nations of the world to gather their armies and their weapons of mass destruction and meet in the Valley of Jezreel.

- The sixth vial of destruction will result in the water flow in the great Euphrates River being shut off so the armies and weapons of the nations to the east will be able to easily and quickly make their way to the staging ground in the Valley of Jezreel.

- Near the end of the seven year invasion the headquarters of the Antichrist, "that great city" will be destroyed by a great fire in one hour.

18

ARMAGEDDON

$\mathcal{B}$y the time the hands on the "Doomsday Clock" signify the human race has only a few days remaining before destruction, the earth will be a tattered smoking shell of the beautiful planet it was just seven years earlier. There will only be a fraction of the world's population remaining alive. Almost every square mile of the earth will exhibit deep scars as a result of the blistering invasion. A toxic haze will hang over the gutted landscape due to the fires, wars, nuclear explosions and devastation from the bombardment of flaming meteors and asteroids. It will seem as though the planet is drenched in blood. The infrastructures of once prosperous highly industrialized nations throughout the world will be almost non-existent leaving the remaining panic-stricken population of the world suffering, starving and having little hope of survival. The astounding number of dead will continue to mount with every tick of the "Doomsday Clock." Can it possibly get any worse? Absolutely! Mankind's genius, technology and modern weapons of mass destruction will prove to be absolutely futile when used against the supernatural power of the universe in the war that will end the world as we know it.

SPECTATORS

THE LAST DAY

As mankind rushes to the edge of destiny and the end of the world the remaining narrative of John may seem impossible to believe if not at least unimaginable. Many of the events John describes are beyond our comprehension and the imagination of mortal man since it exists in the supernatural dimension of the spiritual world.

John's mind was still fixated on the aftermath of the spectacular destruction of "that great city." This time traveler from the past could not possibly comprehend the magnitude of the destruction he had just witnessed. He could only imagine how many people must have burned to death in the horrendous inferno as the entire city disappeared from the face of the earth in just one hour. As the ruins of the city continued to smolder and the smoke from the obliterated capital of evil blanketed the skies, John's attention was drawn back to an area in heaven that was suddenly bustling with activity. He saw a man in heaven he recognized. It was Jesus, the Son of God and his best friend during the brief thirty-three years that He lived on the earth. In fact, John was still taking care of Jesus' mother, Mary, before his exile to Patmos. She moved to Ephesus in what is now modern-day Turkey after the Romans executed her Son. History documents the death of Jesus as well as His miraculous resurrection three days later. After He visited with friends for forty days, he supernaturally ascended to heaven in view of a crowd of witnesses. Now you know it was not coincidental or a random selection that John was chosen above all others to receive the amazing insider information about the end of the world. God chose His Son's best friend to be the recipient of this historic life-saving message for mankind.

It seemed Jesus was personally taking control of the last stage of the invasion. Those in heaven were being directed to an area filled with herds of outstanding supernatural white horses, hundreds of millions of them, waiting patiently for their riders. As Jesus mounted His own magnificent white steed, His eyes were blazing like fire reflecting the intensity of His desire to make the appointment with mankind and the end of the world. When all was ready, Jesus mounted His horse and bolted out of heaven without a word. The saints in heaven followed, each dressed in fine white linen and riding a splendid white horse. John quickly realized he was a witness to the unbelievably powerful spiritual force of the universe that the world's armies were about to confront in the last moments of the invasion. Even though the great number of saints on white horses will undoubtedly be intimidating to the humans, only Jesus will actually meet the challenge of the armies of the world. The saints will only be spectators. John noticed that Jesus was wearing crowns of victory, signifying the epic battle of Armageddon and the war of the worlds was won before it ever began.[1]

"COME AND GET IT!"

As the military personnel completed the assembly of troops, equipment and weapons in the Valley of Jezreel near Mount Megiddo, John saw an angel standing alone in the glare of the blistering desert sun. The angel cried with a loud voice and supernaturally summoned birds of prey from all over the world to come and feast on the bodies of the soon-to-be dead armies of the Antichrist.[2]

It's as if the angel rang a mystical dinner bell for the birds to "come and get it!" Buzzards, vultures, hawks and every other bird of prey known to man began arriving for the largest buffet in the history of the world. Have you ever seen buzzards flying high in the sky circling over a dead or dying animal? These birds have keen eyesight and smell and an even better sense of a victim's pending death. Once they spot their vulnerable prey, they patiently circle the area and protect their place in line until nature sets the table and dinner is served.

The sun will be obliterated and the sky will be darkened with the number of birds circling high above the armies in the Middle East as the soldiers make last minute preparations for battle. The dark cloud of predators will present an ominous omen of defeat to the armies. Even the birds know who the victor of this battle will be! And when the birds are finished with this meal, there will be millions of other dead around the world for them to feast on!

12:00 PM   THE LAST SIX HOURS

As Jesus makes His way to the battlefield, His first stop will be Edom. In the last days, the armies of the Antichrist will discover the hiding place of the Jews and attack the remnant who escaped the assault on Israel. "The Lord first goes to Edom to rescue Israel from the hands of the Antichrist…"[3] Jesus will win a valiant victory at Edom as blood from the massacred armies of the Antichrist splatters onto his clothes. The remnant of the Jews will escape unharmed and the Antichrist will flee to the Valley of Jezreel to the armies waiting on his command.

The world is on the precipice of destruction as the minutes pass slowly for the battalions of soldiers sweating in the desert heat. Try to imagine what the last hours of life on earth may be like as the armies prepare for the final battle in the following scenario.

After defeating the Antichrist at Edom and rescuing the Jewish remnant, Jesus will continue on to the Valley of Jezreel near Mount Megiddo where the vast armies of the world are waiting impatiently to launch their attack against the unknown invaders. As dawn breaks and the desert sun burns brightly, all the military forces will be in their places. The skies will be eerily vacant of anything but the birds circling high above waiting on dinner. The enormous number of sophisticated radar installations vigilantly scanning the skies for the invaders will detect only an occasional lone military aircraft on the way to the designated staging area.

The commanders of the military forces will speculate on when the invaders will appear and from which direction they will come. They do not have any idea what to expect although they anticipate an attack from the air. The Antichrist will give them little information because he alone knows the power of the One they will be up against. If the armies knew more about the opponent, they would not even be there! The landscape of the Middle East baking in the desert sun will be deathly quiet. There will be no natural disasters and all bombardment from space will have ceased. It's truly the calm before the storm. Where are the invaders? The clock is ticking! Then the silence will be broken by news on radio and television of the massive slaughter of the armies of the Antichrist in Jordan (Edom). Of course, the Antichrist will give quite a different account of the battle when he arrives in the valley so as not to discourage the commanders of the troops. Suddenly, the clocks strike twelve! It is high noon on the last day of life for the human race and it will be the beginning of the longest six hours of terrifying destruction and massacre of humanity ever imagined, the "battle of the great day of God Almighty," Armageddon.

Suddenly the sun will begin to grow dark as if there was a full solar eclipse.[4] Shadows of rocket launchers standing tall in the dazzling sunlight will grow dim and then disappear shrouded in the darkness blanketing the desert landscape. Personnel will struggle to quickly activate temporary lights as they stumble in the darkness. Then the moon will turn blood red giving everything an eerie reflection of imminent death.[5] The screens of radar installations that have been relentlessly scanning the heavens to no avail will suddenly "light up" brightly with thousands of strange-looking unidentifiable images not yet visible to the personnel on the ground. The military leaders will be baffled, frightened and panic-stricken by the number of indications on the radar. It will look like a host of invaders swooping in from every direction. Little do the armies know that the vast fleet of alien-looking objects will simply watch silently from the nearby airspace. Unexpectedly, the image of only one "blip" on the radar screen is seen descending toward them from the legion of objects in the sky. In a backdrop of darkness the presumed target is a blinding light.[6] The world's armed forces will be unable to see the target in their sights. His power will radiate out in all directions striking fear in the hearts of all. The armies of the earth will quickly realize the overwhelming force of the One they are going against. They have been deceived again by the Antichrist, but it's too late to turn back!

THE EARTH'S LAST STAND

The vast armies made up of millions of soldiers will stand traumatized at the sight of Jesus. They will notice their intended target has the supernatural power to descend from the heavens without the aid of any kind of propulsion and he doesn't appear to have any weapons. He doesn't even have any visible body armor for protection! The armies will likely conclude that this being must have some type of cosmic force shield to stand unarmed in the sights of all their sophisticated weapons. They will have no choice but to try and make a pre-emptive strike and launch their weapons of mass destruction. Then as weapons are carelessly deployed at the "target" as a result of panic and confusion, Jesus will simply speak words of death to the armies of the rebellious nations, and they will be destroyed. His words will strike the troops like a sharp sword instantaneously severing the life from each soldier and setting the dinner table for the waiting predators.[7]

We're not told exactly how the armies will be destroyed when Jesus strikes them. However, the ancient manuscripts do offer some very graphic clues to the death of the soldiers. Many of the men and women will die a horrifying death with their flesh rotting and falling from their bodies, eyes decaying in their sockets and tongues disintegrating in their mouths before they even fall to the ground.[8] The battleground will look like something out of a science fiction movie. Human flesh will drip from bodies like wax melting from life-size mannequins in a raging fire. Imagine the air thick with screams for help from men and women as their bodies disintegrate. The air will be filled with the pungent odor of burning flesh.

This horrendous agonizing attack sounds like the results of severe radiation burns due to nuclear explosions at close range. It may be nervous "trigger-happy" soldiers that launch nuclear warheads within their ranks destroying their own troops in the confusion. Perhaps the overwhelming power of the devastating strike by Jesus will detonate the nuclear weapons and other weapons of mass destruction prematurely. The dreadful mushroom cloud characteristic of nuclear explosions will be all too common in the last hours. The results will be shocking, and the fatalities among the armies will be massive. Many of the soldiers will attempt to flee the battlefield only to be stopped dead in their tracks. The squadrons of attack aircraft will sit idle on the runway with the pilots dead at the controls. Navy warships in the Mediterranean Sea will drift aimlessly without crews and never having fired a shot.

SIX FEET DEEP IN BLOOD

John used the example of a winepress to describe the mind-boggling extent of the horrifying slaughter of the armies. In John's first century world people crushed grapes by trampling them with their feet in large barrels. The juice of the crushed grapes ran out of a hole in the barrel and was collected in earthen jars. However, John said in this case the grapes were trampled in the "winepress outside the city of Jerusalem," only it's the bodies of the soldiers that are crushed, not grapes, and it's the blood of the soldiers' bodies that runs onto the desert floor, not juice. John said the blood from the millions of dead soldiers was four to six feet deep in the valley for a distance of approximately 200 miles.[9] You are probably thinking what a devastating, unimaginable massacre of human beings, but how could there possibly be that much blood? Good question? Here is the answer.

The rest of the world watching the disturbing events by television will realize the battle is lost and the earth and all the inhabitants are doomed! The world will resort to an uncontrolled panic-stricken frenzy not knowing what to do or which way to turn. Of course, many on the battlefield as well as those watching by television will realize this supernatural being must be the God of the universe that they had heard about but refused to believe.

MANGLED CORPSES

IT IS FINISHED

After an overwhelming triumphant victory over the armies in the Valley of Jezreel and later in the Valley of Jehoshaphat, Jesus will proceed to Jerusalem for the final battle. The Antichrist and what is left of the world's armies will storm the city of Jerusalem making one last attempt to destroy the crown jewel of Israel. However, Jesus will arrive in time to totally decimate the armies as He did in the other confrontations. With another incredible "out of this world" display of phenomenal power, Jesus will reign victorious again. The earthly armies of the Antichrist will be defeated with mangled corpses littering the landscape. When the battles of Armageddon are finished, the seventh angel will release the last vial of destruction to finish off the human race. There will still be countless people throughout the world who witnessed the destruction of Armageddon by television but still refuse the gift of life.

As the contents of the last vial are poured on to the earth a great earthquake of a magnitude never experienced by mankind begins to literally shake the planet. The massive quake will split the city of Jerusalem into three parts, and cause buildings in cities of nations all over the world to be inundated and collapse crushing their occupants.[10] People everywhere will be screaming for someone to rescue them but no one will come. Every island that has not already been destroyed will be lost beneath the seas. Every mountain that has not already been moved will be reduced to level ground. Once the shaking of the earth diminishes and eventually ceases, there will not likely be a structure of any kind standing anywhere.

SIXTY POUND ICE MISSILES

Finally, there will be an incredible "rain of supernatural hail."[11] A talent, which was an ancient measure of weight, is approximately sixty pounds and the manuscripts indicate each hailstone will weigh one talent. Therefore, anyone caught in the relentless "shower" of sixty-pound ice missiles rocketing down from the heavens will certainly be killed. In addition, each one of these massive hailstones will contain more than seven gallons of water and will melt quickly in the desert heat. As these hailstones melt they will add billions of gallons of water to mix with the blood pouring from the mounds of corpses. With this phenomenal "rain of supernatural hail," the valley will rapidly fill with a mixture of blood and water to the depth described by John. Once the desert sand soaks up the blood and water, the birds of prey that have been patiently circling the battleground will settle down onto the blood drenched desert and begin to feast on the bodies of the dead.

RETURN TO EARTH

Finally, we come to the most dramatic moment in history as Jesus proceeds to the Mount of Olives for His return to earth. More than two thousand years ago a group of people were gathered at the Mount of Olives just a short distance outside the city of Jerusalem. The scene took place about forty days after the supernatural resurrection of Jesus. His closest followers and friends stood sadly by as they watched Him supernaturally ascend from the Mount of Olives into the heavens and disappear into the clouds. However, two angels standing nearby reminded the onlookers that He would return someday to the exact same place he left.[12] Of course, those people had no idea that His return to the Mount of Olives would be two thousand years in the future.

The manuscripts indicate that when the feet of Jesus touch the summit of the Mount of Olives in His descent from heaven, the entire mountain will cataclysmically split into two geographical parts along an east-west line.[13] Although this could certainly happen supernaturally, there is a known east-west geological fault line in the Mount of Olives which could be the catalyst to split the mountain naturally.

THE FINAL CURTAIN CALL

Although the battle of Armageddon will take place only in the Middle East in Jordan, and between Jerusalem and the Valley of Jezreel, the devastating effects to mankind from the return of Jesus will be felt by everyone throughout the world. As soon as Jesus makes His debut in the skies over the Middle East, the entire planet will begin to acknowledge His awesome supernatural power. Imagine what life may be like on earth as the last sands of time fall through the hourglass of humanity. This will be the final curtain call for all who accept the gift of life. For all others the curtain will come down on the stage for the human race. This is the end.

The great earthquake with its epicenter in Jerusalem will destroy the cities and towns still standing around the world and take the lives of most of the occupants. The winds aloft will have carried the deadly clouds of radiation from nuclear explosions throughout the world, blanketing the landscape and sealing the destiny of many others. People throughout the world who survived the earthquakes, storms, meteor strikes and lack of food and water will die a slow, agonizing death from radiation poisoning. However, there will still be people who escaped death, but not for long!

As Jesus descended from the heavens over Jerusalem, John saw lightning bolts electrifying the atmosphere around the world with deafening thunder.[14] The remaining population will panic when they see the massive lightning flashes encircling the planet and dancing wildly, uncontrollably across the landscape. The violent display of deadly electricity unlike anything ever seen before will disrupt the already scarce communication systems and isolate people in distress. Many will die instantly as relentless lightning bolts strike buildings, cars, and homes. The panic in the world will be totally unmanageable. The few survivors will attack and kill each other. It will be as if everyone has gone "mad."[15] The entire world will be subjected to this unbelievable electrifying phenomenon and it won't stop until the lives of all those who ultimately rejected the gift of life are taken in an unspeakable death.

6:00 PM   THE END

It is six o'clock in the Middle East. Six excruciating hours after Armageddon begins the trauma will cease and the earth will again become eerily, deathly quiet. Soon the darkness will begin to subside and the natural light of the sun and moon will return.[16] The daylight will reveal the land littered with the corpses of the world's armies floating in a "sea of blood" as the flocks of birds of prey finish their dinner. There will also be thousands of "lifeless" robots, clones of the Antichrist, standing motionless without the energizing power of Satan in the shattered "Information Centers" throughout the world. They are the only remaining testament of the futile diabolical agenda of the great dictator of the modern world, the Antichrist. The "Doomsday Clock" has stopped again, this time for good! With the battle against the earthly armies majestically won by Jesus and all those who rejected the gift of life destroyed, the Antichrist will be taken with his partner in crime, the Minister of Propaganda, to a fate worse than death for all eternity.[17] Satan will soon join them. There will be no one left alive on earth who ultimately rejected the gift of life. What happens now?

REFLECTIONS

- At high noon on the last day of the existence of the human race, the earth will begin to experience the most horrifying six hours in the history of the world.

- Jesus will descend from heaven with his army of saints dressed in white and mounted on magnificent white horses and proceed to the hiding place of the Jews. There He will gloriously defeat the armies of the Antichrist.

- Jesus will then proceed to the Valleys of Megiddo and Jehoshaphat and destroy all the armies of rebellious mankind gathered in the Middle East in an overwhelming victory.

- Finally, Jesus will meet the Antichrist and the last of his armies at Jerusalem for one last stand. After a magnificent victory by Jesus, the birds of prey will feast on the remains.

- The release of the seventh and last vial of destruction will result in a massive earthquake that will split the city of Jerusalem into three parts. Hailstones weighing sixty pounds will rain down and kill many of those who rejected the gift of life.

- Blood from the massacre of the armies will run through the valley at an incredible depth of four to six feet for approximately 200 miles.

- After declaring victory over the armies of the earth, Jesus will proceed to the Mount of Olives. This is the location of His glorious second coming. The mountain will split in two pieces when His feet touch the summit.

- The only survivors of the invasion will be those who accepted the gift of life.

- At six o'clock in the evening in the Middle East the battle of Armageddon will cease and with the exception of those who possessed the gift of life, humanity will have been extinguished.

- The Antichrist and his Minister of Propaganda will be taken away to their fate worse than death. Satan will soon join them.

The conclusion of many good fiction books may end with a statement that "the realistic accounts of the future dramatized in the book <u>could</u> happen someday." However, the shocking narrative of the future you just read <u>is true and it will happen someday!</u>

You have just read an eye-witness account of the most terrifying seven years of death and suffering in the history of mankind climaxing with Armageddon, the greatest massacre of human life in world history and it only lasted six hours. The good news is it has not happened yet although it may begin at any time. There is no reason for anyone to be left on earth to live through the end of the world after the "Chosen" are evacuated to safety.

Is the insider information that is embraced by historical documents and supported by current world events compelling enough to interest you in learning the secret to surviving the end of the world? Do you really want to take a chance and believe that the end of the world as described herein is just too unimaginable to happen as predicted? What do you have to lose? Everything! Take a few more minutes and turn the page; you will be glad you did.

19

THE KEY TO
THE SECRET

*J*n the next few pages you will discover how to obtain
the gift of life and the key to the secret to surviving the
invasion of earth, Armageddon and the end of the world.
However, let me first introduce you to the one who was
personally responsible for giving us the incredible gift of life
almost 2,000 years ago.

WE'RE ALWAYS ON HIS MIND

He is famous worldwide and has a following of hundreds
of millions of people. As an accomplished authority on life
and living, he holds the secret to having an abundant life
filled with purpose regardless of circumstances. Recognized
as a legendary physician, He is able to heal the deathly ill
against all odds, restore life when the heart stops beating,
enable the lame to walk and return sight to the blind. This
gifted benefactor was the first to implement a privately

funded program to "feed the hungry" by providing food to thousands of people on a crowded hillside in Israel. His financial planning principles have rescued countless families from bankruptcy and helped others to find financial independence. His remarkable counsel restores happiness to those who are desperate and have given up on life, heals failing marriages, helps wayward children find their way home, gives hope to the hopeless and provides a purpose for living to those who have none. He has literally transformed the lives and altered the futures of people around the world for the better while performing all of His work at no charge to the recipient.

This miracle worker was raised by hard-working blue collar parents and had no formal education. As a boy, He amazed everyone with his knowledge. He taught the teachers of His day as a young boy before embarking on a full time career dedicated to helping others. He is still in business today, is available to talk with you and has time to listen to anything you have to say. He cares about what you do and your well-being. We're always on His mind even when we're sleeping. Let me introduce you to Jesus Christ, the Son of God who personally delivered the gift of life to mankind and was the architect of the sacred group of people called the "Chosen" almost 2,000 years ago. You may know them better as Christians. Yes, this is the same Jesus, John's best friend, who will victoriously defeat the earthly armies at Armageddon. Spend a few minutes to learn about the brief life of Jesus on earth and prepare to discover the key to secrets that will change your life forever!

NO ROOM IN THE INN

God delivered the solution to all our problems more than 2,000 years ago in a simple makeshift barn for animals hollowed out of a cave just outside the tiny town of Bethlehem in ancient Israel.[1] He delivered His gift of life to the world with the birth of Jesus Christ, the irrefutable undeniable only Son of God in a stable because there was no room in the nearby overcrowded inn. It's the only "baby shower" where the baby brought the gift. He was greeted at birth only by His earthly parents, Mary and Joseph, and the stable animals.

People flocked to the tiny town at this time of the year to pay their taxes and be counted in the census required by Caesar Augustus and the Roman government. However, the crowds were too busy to notice the birth of a baby boy who would change the world forever. We may criticize the innkeeper because he didn't provide Mary with a room to have the baby, but are we really any different today?

> *No, things really haven't changed much in the last 2,000 years. Most of us are still too busy. The cities, homes, and peoples' lives are still too crowded with festivities at Christmas, the day that we celebrate His birthday. Shopping malls are packed at Christmas with people spending money they don't have for gifts people don't need, sometimes don't even want and probably won't remember in a few weeks. We remember the season, but do we pay any attention to the reason for the season?*

There has never been another person before or after who has made such an impact on peoples' lives as Jesus. However, in spite of all Jesus did for others during His brief life on earth, he was accused of blasphemy by the religious leaders of His day because He was considered a threat to their livelihood.

As a result, He was executed on a Roman cross at the young age of thirty three. Even though Jesus died at the hands of the Romans, his execution was given the overwhelming approval of crowds made up of the very people that He healed, fed, and ministered to during his brief life on earth.

You might say Jesus was sentenced to death by a disappointed crowd of followers. The Jews had hoped for a revolutionary to come and save them from the brutal reign of the Romans, but God gave them a gentle man with compassion for people. The crowds wanted a king to reign over an earthly kingdom where they could live happily ever after, but God gave the world a man who would willingly forfeit his life rather than fight so that others may live. Those who listened to the prophets expected a knight in shining armor to arrive on a galloping white steed armed with weapons for battle with the Roman soldiers. Instead, Jesus rode a lowly donkey into Jerusalem with only the clothes on His back. The disappointed followers didn't receive what they wanted or expected. They were given what they needed, the gift of life that provided a real purpose for living and the promise of eternity in heaven after death. This gift also provided the secret to survival for a future generation that would be targeted for destruction by the invasion of the planet.

THE KEY TO THE SECRET

The key to the secret of the gift of life and the only way to survive the end of the world are included in the collection of inerrant ancient manuscripts inspired by God that contain the insider information. We know this collection of manuscripts as Scriptures in the best-selling book called the *Holy Bible.* The insider information describing the events leading to Armageddon and the end of the world is better known as the Tribulation and is contained in the elusive book known as *Revelation*-the last book in the *Bible.*

To obtain the key to the secret of the gift of life and the only way to survive the end of the world follow the simple instructions from the *Bible*. First, one should recognize that every person is born with a fundamental nature to follow his or her own will and the belief that each knows better than anyone else what is best for them. Of course, this instinctive characteristic that often motivates unfavorable behavior is stronger in some people than in others and often destroys their lives as well as the lives of loved ones and even innocent bystanders. Parents learn that children do not have to be taught to misbehave, steal, lie, or be selfish from the first day they cry for attention. Would you agree that people don't have to be taught to be disobedient, insubordinate or defiant to authority? The overcrowded prisons are proof of that fact.

Admit that you have sinned and fallen short of the best in life that God desires for you.[2]

If the fundamental nature of mankind drives unfavorable behavior, what is sin? Sin is not a "religious word" of accusation but rather a Greek word that was applied to an archer when he missed the target with his arrow. To sin simply means missing the mark of being everything that God wants a person to be. Parents want their children to have everything they need to be happy and successful. However, sometimes children stray from the wisdom and principles of life taught by their parents because of their fundamental sin nature. As they reject the training of their parents, they miss the mark or fall short of the life the parents hoped for and tried to provide for them. Similarly, God's desire for mankind to have a life with real purpose as well as a meaningful relationship with Him is often hampered by the fundamental sin nature we are all born with.

You may be thinking, "I'm not perfect but I'm a good person. I work hard, pay my taxes and abide by the law. I haven't done anything that would cause me to be arrested and go to jail. How could I have committed a sin or done anything that God is unhappy with?" Missing the mark or sin does not necessarily manifest itself in crimes punishable by the criminal court system. Consider the divine Biblical principles or Ten Commandments given to us by God upon which our laws are based. If you have ever told a lie, stretched the truth, took something that didn't belong to you, or worshipped anything or anybody other than God you have missed the mark God has for your life. It means there is a vacuum in your life that prevents you from being completely happy and content regardless of your circumstances. This vacuum may manifest itself as unhappiness, lack of purpose, or discontent with life and self. However, the true source of those feelings may not be understood. It doesn't mean you're a bad person; you're just not taking advantage of the best life God wants for you and God will fill the vacuum. Unfortunately, God also established a penalty that must be paid for sin.

Recognize that "death" is the penalty for sin but the gift of life assures you eternal life in heaven through the sacrifice of Jesus. [3]

Parents simply place their disobedient children in "time out" for a short while until behavior improves. The criminal justice system places people convicted of crimes in prison for a period commensurate with the crime. On the contrary, the innate sin nature of mankind that provides the potential for misguided behavior cannot be eradicated or cancelled by good parents with a positive home life, a favorable environment, a better job or even incarceration with rehabilitation. Only God can supernaturally alter the fundamental sin nature of mankind. In addition, the penalty or price for sin, eternity in a place of spiritual darkness and torment called hell must be paid by someone. Hell is not a myth it is a very real place as real as heaven. This is "death" following the physical death of a person on earth. Thankfully, there is a way we can avoid paying the penalty of sin ourselves!

God loved you so much regardless of your behavior and your past that he gave his only son Jesus to die in your place, pay the penalty and offer you a complete pardon for sin. You no longer owe God anything for whatever you have done or ever will do. The bill has been paid in full if you accept the pardon.[4]

Before Jesus, the only way the penalty for sin against God could be paid was with the shed blood of a sacrificial lamb or other "perfect animal." However, the sacrificial process requiring priests and a holy altar had to be repeated over time because mankind continued to sin. He couldn't help it; it was his "sin nature" and the sacrifice of an animal didn't change this nature. As a result of the grace of God, Jesus became the ultimate perfect "sacrificial lamb" on a Roman cross to end the system of sacrifices and provide the gift of life, an irrevocable pardon for sin forever for anyone who would accept it.

On the day Jesus was executed in the same way as a common criminal, no one actually knew why Jesus had to die. He hung on a cross bearing the gift of life for all humanity and the scars of death from His disappointed followers. He could have called legions of angels from heaven to free him from the cross and destroy the perpetrators. But He didn't! The price for the pardon of our sins could only be paid by a supernatural, sacrificial act of God. If Jesus is dead, there would be no supernatural act of sacrifice and His death would have been as insignificant as the death of every other great prophet of the past. However, three days after He was pronounced dead by the Roman soldiers, Jesus was supernaturally and miraculously resurrected. He visited and ate with friends and followers for forty days and then mysteriously ascended to heaven. Unlike all other religious leaders of the past, present and future, Jesus is alive today!

This gift is available today and will give you a complete pardon from the consequences of all sin. This amazing gift of life erases everything in your past that is undesirable and unacceptable to God. It "wipes the slate clean," fills the soul with the pure spirit of God and provides forgiveness for sins past, present and future.

**The cross is
The key
To the secret
To surviving the End of the World.**

THE KEY

The 170 foot high Cross at Sagemont Church, Houston, Texas
Photograph by J.E. Bouvier

The gift of life is available only because of the grace of God through faith in Jesus. Although grace cannot be understood, it can be expressed this way: **G**od's **R**iches **A**t **C**hrist's **E**xpense.

Believe that the gift of life comes only through faith and trust in Jesus by the grace of God. It's a gift that cannot be bought or earned by being a good person.[5]

Believe in your heart that Jesus died for you and that God raised him from the dead and you will receive the gift of life. [6]

Now you can have the gift of life and seal your final destination in eternity by praying this simple prayer.

Thank you God for sending your Son Jesus to die for my sins, and I believe in my heart that he is alive today! Please forgive me for all the things I have done that are displeasing to you. I'm sorry for the sin in my life. I only want my life to please you and honor you in everything I do from this moment on. Take control of my life and guide me in every step I take. Thank you for your amazing grace of forgiveness. Thank you for the gift of eternal life. I will trust you for everything in my life. Now I know the secret of the only way to escape the coming invasion of earth; if I am alive at that time, Jesus will come for me and remove me from this earth to safety!

By praying the simple prayer above God assures you:

- forgiveness of all sin, past present and future
- everlasting life in heaven the instant your life on earth ends

- a more meaningful purpose-filled life on earth starting today
- lifetime membership in the " Chosen"
- rescues you from the earth to safety before the invasion of earth begins if you're living in the "terminal generation"
- the gift of life and its promises can never be lost under any circumstances.[7]
- the secrets to successful living

If there had been any other way, God would not have let His Son suffer and
Jesus wouldn't have died.
But there wasn't and so He did.
No one understands it.
No one deserves it.
Everyone needs it but
You can't earn it,
You can't beg or plead for it,
You can't buy it and
You can't work for it.
You only need to accept it.
It's a gift from God.
It's the wonderful, amazing grace of God.
It's the gift that keeps on giving for eternity,
But why would God allow his only Son to die for you and me?
No one knows,
It's just God's amazing love. It's a love for you and me that will always be a mystery.

FIVE SECRETS TO SUCCESSFUL LIVING

Once you accept the gift of life learn the following five secrets to have total success in life:

- acknowledge God in everything you do,
- trust God for everything you need,
- worship God regularly,
- serve others and
- return to God part of the success He gives you.

WHAT ABOUT CHILDREN?

You may wonder why the children were taken with the "Chosen" before the invasion began. Children are very special to God. Any child that dies before he or she understands the gift of life and has an opportunity to accept the gift is assured of spending eternity in heaven. Therefore, any child living in the "terminal generation" will be taken with the "Chosen" to safety before the invasion begins.[8]

WHY MUST THE EARTH SUFFER THE INVASION?

Many will question why the earth must suffer through such a horrific invasion. However, by now you may realize the reason for the deadly encounter with mankind. God wants His creation to look to Him, trust Him and love Him. After centuries of humanity turning its back on God and abusing His Son, the massive invasion of earth will provide a last opportunity to persuade mankind in a most unusual way to seek the Creator. God continues to delay the invasion in the hope that many more people will come to the life-saving realization that they must accept the gift of life.

"THE CHURCH"

If you prayed a prayer believing in your heart that Jesus died for your sins and trusting God to forgive you and change your life forever, He did! You are now a "lifetime member" of the sacred group called the "Chosen" or better known today as "The Church." Of course, people have many different opinions about the church and what it stands for because most people don't know the truth about "The Church."

The word church may stir your memory of a stuffy group of "Bible thumpers" that you encountered on a chance visit to a service at the repeated request of your mother or spouse on a special occasion. You may have attended a tent revival where an evangelist preached for what seemed like an eternity knowing it may be his only shot preaching to some people about hellfire and brimstone. On the other hand, the word church may remind you of a small building with a steeple and a cross on top. You may remember spending one or two weeks of your summers as a child in what was called Vacation Bible School. There you may have made projects like carving objects out of bars of ivory soap or making prints of your small hands in plaster of Paris that were cherished by your parents. You learned simple songs and memory verses that were etched in your mind and still bring back special memories of those days. Whatever your experiences with the organized church, put them aside and look at the origin and meaning of "The Church."

Steeple and cross on a small church in Texas
Photograph by J.E. Bouvier

Almost 2,000 years ago Jesus said <u>He</u> would build <u>His</u> "church" and no one would destroy it.[9] Therefore "The Church" belongs to Jesus and religious organizations and denominations belong to the world. "The Church" grew rapidly beginning with the day when more than 3,000 men and many women and children accepted the amazing grace of God and the gift of life provided by the sacrificial death of Jesus on the cross. This was the first congregation of Christians (the "Chosen") who later came to be called "The Church." Originally the congregations had no buildings. The Christians were "The Church" wherever they went and that is still the case today. The ancient manuscripts actually list four characteristics of the first congregation of Christians in "The Church" that should be the model for any congregation of Christians today.[10]

- They were consistent with their attendance in worship.

- They adhered to the fundamental principles and doctrines on which they were established.

- They had regular fellowship together.

- They praised Jesus regularly in prayer and worship.

You don't have to fill out a form, take a number or send in an application for membership in the "The Church." You're a lifetime member the moment you give your life to Jesus. Now you are "The Church" and it goes everywhere you go. Of course, every Christian should find a local congregation where members of "The Church" are present and the *Bible* is believed with commitment and taught without compromise. The characteristics of the congregation documented above should be used as a guide to finding a local church congregation that subscribes to the fundamental beliefs and principles of "The Church."

There is no one affiliation that can claim to be the stronghold for all members of "The Church." They are called Baptists, Catholics, Methodists, as well as other denominations. Unfortunately, not every building with the word church in the name is privileged to have members of "The Church" in their congregation. As a result, when members of the "Chosen," better known today as "The Church" are safely evacuated from earth prior to the invasion, many congregations of churches will be left confused and panic-stricken wondering where did they go wrong with their beliefs.

Thankfully, there are many churches that have maintained a sharp focus on the simple message of Jesus and many pastors continue to untiringly preach the *Bible*, the inerrant, inspired word of God, without compromise year after year. They offer the gift of life through the amazing grace of God as well as warn of the consequence of rejecting God's gift. They minister to the community as well as to the world. Dr. John Morgan, pastor of Sagemont Church in Houston, Texas, where we have attended for almost forty years is a great example.

TWAS THE NIGHT BEFORE CHRISTMAS

We've all enjoyed reading the timeless poem "*Twas the Night before Christmas*" by Clement Clarke Moore. We laugh as the poem describes the surprise of the children at the arrival of Santa in their home even though they are expecting him sometime on Christmas Eve. They just don't know exactly what time he is coming so it will still be a surprise. Unfortunately, if the poem is reworded a little, it can describe what it will be like in the homes of millions of people around the world when the call comes to evacuate

"The Church" from earth to safety. The ancient manuscripts clearly reveal that Jesus will come for "The Church" and take the members to safety before the invasion begins, but He will come when least expected! It will definitely be a surprise! What will it be like in your home?

Twas the Night Before Jesus Came

Twas the night before Jesus came and all through the house
Not a creature was praying, not one in the house,
Their Bibles were lain on the shelf without care
In hopes that Jesus would not come there,

The children were dressing to crawl into bed
Not once ever kneeling or bowing a head.
And Mom in her rocker with baby on her lap
Was watching the late show while I took a nap,

When out of the East there arose such a clatter,
I sprang to my feet to see what was the matter,
Away to the window I flew like a flash
Tore open the shutters and threw up the sash.

When what to my wondering eyes should appear
But angels proclaiming that Jesus was here,
With a light like the sun sending forth a bright ray
I knew in a moment this must be THE DAY!

The light of His face made me cover my head
It was Jesus returning just like He had said,
And though I possessed worldly wisdom and wealth,
I cried when I saw Him in spite of myself,

In the Book of Life which He held in His hand
Was written the name of every saved man,

He spoke not a word as HE searched for my name;
When He said, "It's not here," my head hung in shame,
The people whose names had been written with Love
He gathered to take to His Father above,
With those who were ready He rose without a sound
While all of the rest were left standing around,

I fell to my knees, but it was too late;
I had waited too long and thus sealed my fate,
I stood and I cried as they rose out of sight;
Oh, if only I had been ready tonight,

In the words of this poem the meaning is clear;
The coming of Jesus is drawing near,
There's only one life and when comes the last call
We'll find the Bible was true after all![11]

Dianne Frances Donenfield

Any delay in making the decision to accept the gift of life may ultimately jeopardize your ability to escape the imminent invasion of earth climaxing with Armageddon and subjecting you to suffering and pain as the world skids to an end. If you miss the evacuation of "The Church," you will be left on earth to suffer during the invasion but you may have another opportunity to accept the gift of life before it's too late. However, if you die without possessing the gift of life, you are doomed to face the ultimate judgment of God and spend eternity in darkness and torment in hell with absolutely no recourse! Death may come at any moment, unannounced and without warning, to any one of us and time may be running out. Our days are numbered; we just don't know the number.

John's journey to the future ends with both bad news and good news!

The bad news! For those who choose not to accept the gift of life for any reason prior to their death, discover the next bloodcurdling scene that they are destined to experience. You won't believe it!

The good news! For those who possess this gift of life and are heaven bound, catch a glimpse of what their wonderful final destination in eternity will be like. You won't believe it, but you will be excited about it!

20

TICK, TOCK...

TIME MAY BE RUNNING OUT

*O*n January 15, 2009, 155 passengers and crew on US Airways Flight 1549 left La Guardia Airport in New York City and anticipated arriving at their scheduled destination on time. However, shortly after taking off, the plane was exposed to a bizarre, unprecedented, multiple bird strike that disabled and shut down both jet engines. In the next few minutes, the experienced pilot executed a masterfully "controlled crash landing" in the Hudson River. Many, if not most, of those on board likely believed they would die in what looked like an imminent disaster. But they didn't! In fact, due to the heroic efforts of the captain and other crew on board, every single person was spared a watery grave. God intervened in that troubled flight for some unknown reason and miraculously extended the time on earth for each of those on board that aircraft. Perhaps, God gave those who had not already accepted the gift of life another opportunity. Unfortunately, that's not always the case and time may be running out!

Consider the tragedy of the space shuttle Columbia. I didn't know any of the seven astronauts personally but Evelyn Husband, the wife of Rick Husband, Commander of the Columbia, is a member of our church in Houston, Texas. She recently gave her testimony, as well as that of her husband, which is clearly expressed in her book *High Calling*. This book documents the life of Rick Husband and his career as a pilot for the military and for NASA. Both Evelyn and Rick accepted God's gift of life years earlier. Evelyn included in her book an excerpt from the special instructions that Rick gave in the event of his death. This was a routine document prepared by each of the astronauts before flying into space. "In this section, Rick wrote 'Tell em about Jesus!-That He is *real* to me. *Proverbs 3:5-6, Colossians 3:23*.' That's what Rick wanted done in case something happened; he wanted people to know about Jesus and His love"[1] We're confident that Rick was in the arms of God the instant the shuttle Columbia gave him up to his final destination in eternity. Rick was prepared even though death came suddenly and without warning. Why didn't God spare the Columbia and crew with a miraculous landing? Had the other crew members accepted the gift of life? Were they prepared for eternity? Unfortunately, everyone who ultimately rejects the gift of life, regardless of the reason, must face the awesome judgment of God someday.

APPOINTMENT WITH GOD

John's attention was suddenly turned to the unavoidable sentencing of all who had chosen to reject God and the gift of life. The spiritual bodies of all those who have ever ultimately rejected God will be brought from hell where their spirit was sent the instant they drew their last breath. It's regrettable that the heartbreaking processional of souls facing this judgment will likely stretch for miles. One by one they will make their inescapable, personal gut wrenching, divine appointment with God. I can't imagine facing our awesome God in what is known as the Great White Throne Judgment. I'm thankful to God that I won't have to, and I pray that you won't either!

I CAN'T FIND YOUR NAME

The sentencing for those who refuse God's pardon for their sin is not going to be a trial by jury with lawyers and appeals and Supreme Court rulings, letters from the Governor's office, or a pardon from the President of the United States. The judgment of God is final!

> *Contrary to what many people say and believe, God does not send people to hell. He freely offers the gift of life and provides a complete pardon from the penalty for sin for anyone who will accept it. However, if a person refuses to accept the pardon that comes with the gift, God has no choice but to sentence him to eternity in hell. Every person has that choice to make.*

When everyone is present and accounted for, God will open two massive sets of books, the Book of Life and the Lamb's Book of Life.[2] Every person's name is written in the Book of Life when they're born. If they refuse to accept God's gift of life by the time of their physical death, their name is removed from the book. Therefore, by the time of the Great White Throne Judgment, the Book of Life will contain only the names of those who accepted the gift of life by the grace of God. Of course, the names of those who lived before the arrival of the gift about two thousand years ago remain in the book based on their trust and faith in God and obedience to His laws. The Lamb's Book of Life, as the name implies, contains only the names of those who have accepted the gift of life provided through Jesus Christ, the sacrificial Lamb of God. As each person surrenders his life to God and accepts the gift of life, he becomes a member of "The Church" and his name is entered in the Lamb's Book of Life. Only the members of "The Church," in other words Christians, are included in this book.

There is no way to comprehend what John describes next but try to imagine a scene like the following.

There will be no jokes about heaven and hell by those waiting for their appointment with God. One by one, each person will humbly approach the throne of God with head bowed when their name is called. They must listen to God as He speaks to them. This may be the first time that many people will actually hear and listen to God speaking directly to them.

Those standing before God will tremble with tears in their eyes as His fingers slowly and meticulously scroll down through the pages of the two books looking for the person's name, pausing momentarily so as not to overlook a name. Sadly, some people know their names won't be found. Others will be convinced they must be in the books because they have been such model citizens all their lives doing good and helping others. As God finally searches all the pages and closes the books, He will look straight into the eyes of each individual and say with great sadness, "I'm sorry, I can't find your name; take him away." God has no choice but to sentence the person to eternity in hell. Without delay, representatives from the prison of darkness will be summoned to take him away to hell. As the evil spirits gleefully drag away the condemned soul screaming for mercy, God will sadly call the next person in line to step up to the throne. Think how long this process will take. However, God and those being sentenced will have nothing but time!

Now for a more pleasant scene for those who are heaven bound and will not have to face the Great White Throne

Judgment of God. One of the most exciting parts of taking a trip to a place we have never been is to learn something about where we're going before we leave.

HEAVEN ON EARTH

First there is a surprise ending to the insider information after Armageddon and the end of the world. The world doesn't actually end!

The smoking shell of a world devastated by the invasion will be wonderfully, supernaturally re-created by God. Then something absolutely spectacular will occur that will astound the "doomsday" prophets of the world. One of the angels involved in the last seven dreadful vials of destruction took John to the top of a high mountain in the Middle East near Jerusalem. There he had a bird's eye view of the dazzling glory of heaven, the holy city Jerusalem, as it descended to the earth. Did you hear that? John witnessed the relocation of heaven to the "new" earth. For the first time in history, there actually will be "heaven on earth."

The angel took a supernatural ruler and measured the dimensions of the city to illustrate how much room there will be for everyone. The angel said the city was 1,500 miles long, 1,500 miles wide and 1,500 miles high. Just imagine one leg of the base of the city would stretch from the Gulf Coast to New York City with a height towering 1,500 miles into space. What a sight this must have been for John! Remember, the space shuttle only travels to an altitude of about 250 miles above earth. You may be concerned about the lack of air and the cold of deep space in the upper reaches of the city. However, that will not be a problem because we will not be the same fragile air-breathing humans we are now. Remember, we will be transformed to wonderful spiritual, heavenly beings.

Before Jesus ascended to heaven almost 2,000 years ago, he told his disciples about mansions in heaven which He was going to prepare for everyone.[3] We all know what a mansion is. It's what most of us enjoy looking at but don't have and can't afford. All believers will have an awesome totally furnished mansion in heaven on earth and there will be room for everyone. God is preparing the very best for us. The city of heaven will have a great wall more than 200 feet high with twelve gates. This wall is not for protection; it's just symbolic of the fact that only those who have their names written in the Book of Life or the Lamb's Book of Life will be able to enter the gates. Each gate in the wall is made of a single pearl, which is difficult to believe. However, everyone will be free to come and go from the city because the gates are never closed. That means you will be able to leave the city and travel anywhere on the new earth as often and as long as you wish which, in fact, may resemble the original Garden of Eden. And what would a city be without streets? John saw at least one street in the city, and it will be paved with pure gold.

God is trying to make a point here. He used gold, the precious metal that mankind worships as one of the most valuable commodities on earth, for building materials in heaven. People struggle and sacrifice their lives and sometimes the lives of their families for possession of gold and other precious metals on earth, but you can't take it with you. Even if you could, the gold would end up as part of the street in heaven. The simple lesson here is to be careful what you invest your life in! In the long run, it may not be what it seems. We should have learned this lesson as a result of the recent meltdown of the global financial markets that began in 2007-2008.

The city itself will also be made of pure gold that is transparent like glass. That means as the saints come and go, they can see what is going on everywhere. It appears there will be no privacy, but there will be no secrets and nothing to hide. John said there was no Temple in the new heaven because God is the Temple. He also mentioned there was no need for the sun or moon because the glory of God will provide the light.

LIFE IN HEAVEN ON EARTH

There will be no night in heaven and no reason to ever go to bed.[4] Do you realize most of us spend more than thirty percent of our life just sleeping, and that does not include time for naps? Our earthly bodies require sleep and rest to recharge and prepare for the next day. Will we require rest in heaven? I know God rested on the seventh day after creating the world. However, I seriously doubt we will be doing any "creating."

You likely have many more questions about heaven. What about our families? If we're married now, will we still be married to our spouse? Will we know our children and friends? Will we wear clothing? There are answers to each of these questions. During the ministry of Jesus on earth, he was asked about marriage in heaven. Religious leaders asked Jesus if a woman had seven husbands on earth, which of the men would be her husband in heaven. Jesus simply explained that there will be no marriage in heaven.[5]

We will not be married, but we will have millions of friends. Will we recognize people? There is a scene in the ancient manuscripts where Peter, one of Jesus' closest disciples, recognized and called by name two prophets, Moses and Elijah, who had both died many years before Peter was born.[6] Therefore, it is highly probable that we will recognize family and friends. We may also have a kind of supernatural recognition of people we have read about like the disciples and prophets of old. Also, there will be no need to worry about what to wear everyday because the fashionable attire will be pure white robes.

Finally, one of the best parts of the promise of eternity in heaven is that there will be no pain, no suffering and no tears. God will wipe away all tears in heaven.[7] There are many people today who have life-threatening and potentially lifelong debilitating diseases that threaten to steal the joy, as well as the years, of their lives on earth. Tears of pain and anguish are a routine part of their day. However, the saints in heaven will discover they have new bodies which are perfect and immune to sickness of every kind. People can throw away the oxygen bottles, the crutches, medicine and all other medical aids.

There are many reasons for tears other than pain. How could we be happy in heaven with the vivid memory of friends or family who rejected the gift of life and are spending eternity in hell? That thought would haunt us forever. When we get to heaven, God will remove any memory that threatens to bring tears which spoil our joy of heaven.[8]

John said he saw a river of crystal clear water that began at the throne of God and ran for as far as you can see. Will there be fish in the river for us to catch and eat? The scriptures are silent on this subject but why not? It does not say where the river goes, but John does tell us there will be a tree on either side of the river. It will have twelve kinds of fruit and yield fruit every month. John also saw angels waving palms. Perhaps there will be palm trees growing near the river. We will probably spend the first one million years or so just thanking God for His grace, touring heaven, meeting friends, and admiring the beauty of our new home.

THE BOTTOM LINE

What's the bottom line! If you're still not sure about the truth that's been revealed to you about Armageddon, the only way to survive the end of the world and your final destination in eternity do not take my word for it. Search the scriptures of the *Bible* where the insider information and the keys to the gift of life are written and discover the truth while there is still time! Your clock is ticking and who knows, your number may be up any minute and your journey on earth will be abruptly terminated. On the other hand, the "Doomsday Clock" may be activated at anytime and you may find that you have been left with only your skepticism and unbelief in the truth of the ancient manuscripts to comfort you.

IS THAT YOUR FINAL ANSWER?

The 170 foot Cross at night at Sagemont Church, Houston, Texas
Photograph by J.E. Bouvier

If you made a decision to accept the gift of life, need prayer for your life or have any other comments about *Escaping Armageddon*, I look forward to hearing from you. Simply email me at my website, www.jamesbouvier.com. God bless you!

NOTES

All Scripture quotations and references are taken from the King James Version of the Holy Bible. Used by permission.

Introduction

Chapter 1 Signs

Chapter 2 The Day We Can Never Forget

1. Photograph of the World Trade Center, New York, City, New York, photographed by copyright-Ken Tannenbaum, L38-287983, AGE Fotostock Rights Managed Photograph.

2. Photograph of The Sphere in Battery Park, New York City, New York, by S Bouvier, Used by Permission.

Chapter 3 We Have Been Warned

1. Photograph of Launch of Columbia, January 16, 2003-NASA File Photograph-not copyrighted. Used by permission, NASA Media Services.

2. Evelyn Husband with Donna Van Liere, Excerpts taken from <u>High Calling</u> (Nashville Tennessee: Thomas Nelson Inc. ,copyright 2003) page 191, Reprinted by permission, all rights reserved.

3. Stephen Walker, Excerpts taken from <u>Shockwave </u>(New York: Harper Collins Publishers, 10 East 53rd Street, New York, NY Copyright 2005), page 157, 160.

4. Ibid., page 319.

Chapter 4 Back 2000 Years to the Future

1. William Barclay, Excerpts taken from <u>The Revelation of John</u>, Volume 1, Revised Edition, (Philadelphia: Westminster John Knox Press, Copyright 1976) page 41,Used by Permission of The Westminster John Knox Press.

2. Photograph of the Island of Patmos, number 1023-8120XC, photographer Randa. Bishop/Fotosearch Copyright 2009.

Chapter 5 Where Did They Go?

1. I Thessalonians 4:17.

2. I Corinthians 15: 52

3. I Thessalonians 4:16

4. Photograph of the illusion of an alien flying saucer in Piraeus, Greece by Sharon Bouvier. Used by Permission.

Chapter 6 The Doomsday Clock

1. Daniel 9:21-27.

2. Stephen R. Miller, excerpts taken from <u>The New American Commentary</u>, Daniel Volume 18, (Nashville Tennessee: Broadman and Holman Publishing Group, copyright 1994), page 257, Used by permission.

3. Ibid., page 263, 266.

4. Ibid., page 268.

Chapter 7 He Will Rule the World

1. Stephen R. Miller, excerpts taken from <u>The New American Commentary, Daniel Volume 18</u>, page 197.

2. Ibid., page 197.

3. Ibid., page 198.

4. Ibid., page 198.

5. Ibid., page 199.

6. Ibid., page 201.

7. Ibid., page 202.

8. Ibid., page 202.

9. Daniel 8: 25.

10. Revelation 6:2.

11. Revelation: 17: 12, 13.

12. Tim La Haye, Excerpts taken from <u>Revelation Illustrated and Made Plain</u> (Grand Rapids Michigan: Zondervan Publishing House of the Zondervan Corporation, Grand Rapids Michigan 49506, Copyright 1977) page 173. Used by permission of Zondervan. (www.zondervan.com).

13. Daniel 8:24.

14. 2 Thessalonians 2: 9; Daniel 11:36; Daniel 8:24; Daniel 7:25; Daniel 11:43; Daniel 8:25.

15. Daniel 8:25.

16. John McCormick, General Editors: Neill Nugent, William E. Paterson, <u>Understanding the European Union</u>, (Palgrave Macmillan Publisher, Houndmills, Basingstoke, Hampshire RG21 2XS, And 175 fifth Avenue, New York, N.Y. 10010, Companies and Representatives throughout the world, Copyright 2005). page 219-220. Reproduced with permission of Palgrave Macmillan.

17. Ibid., page 220.

18. Ibid., page 232.

19. Karel Janicek and William J. Kole, Associated Press, "Obama scrapping missile shield for Czech, Poland" September 17, 2009, (<u>http://www.mysanantonio.com/</u>

military/Obama) Used with permission of The Associated Press Copyright 2009, all rights reserved.

20. Vladimir Isachenkov, Associated Press, "Putin Warns Threat of Sanctions against Iran Could Ruin Talks on Nuclear Program" October 14, 2009, Copyright 2009, all rights reserved (http://www.chicagotribune.com/news/nationworld/sns-) Used with permission of the Associated Press.

21. John McCormick, General Editors: Neill Nugent, William E. Paterson, Understanding the European Union, page 220. Reproduced with permission of Palgrave Macmillan.

22. Ibid., page 226.

23. Ibid., page 76.

24. Ibid., page 233.

25. Christopher S. Rugaber, AP Writer, Associated Press, "Meltdown101: Will China Global Currency Idea Fly?" 3/24/2009 (http://www.newsvine.com/news/2009/03/24/2593397-) Used with permission of The Associated Press. Copyright 2009, All rights reserved.

Chapter 8 You Can Run but You Can't Hide

1. Revelation13:16-18.

2. Stephen A. Brown, excerpts taken from Revolution at the Checkout Counter, (Cambridge Massachusetts and London, England: Harvard University Press, Copyright 1997 by the President and Fellows of Harvard College) page xiii, Used with permission.

3 Ibid., page 9.

4. Revelation 13:16.

5. Associated Press Release, "FDA Approves Computer Chip for Humans" October 13, 2004 (http://www.msnbc.msn.com/id/6237364/) page ¼. Used with permission of The Associated Press, Copyright 2009. All rights reserved.

6. Ibid., page 2/4.

1. Ezekiel 36: 24.

2. Tim La Haye and Ed Hinson, excerpts taken from <u>Global Warming:</u> Are We on the Brink of World War III? (Eugene, Oregon, 97402: Tim La Haye Ministries, la Haye Publishing Group, LLC and Ed Hinson Published by Harvest House Publishers, Copyright 2007), Page 125. www.harvesthousepublishers.com. Used with Permission of Harvest House Publishers.

3. Matthew 24.

4. Ezekiel 38, 39.

5. John F. Walvoord with Mark Hitchcock, excerpts taken from <u>Armageddon, Oil and Terror,</u> (Carol Stream Illinois: by JFW Publishing Trust Copyright 2007). page 94.Used by permission of Tyndale House Publishers, Inc, All rights reserved,

6. Joel C. Rosenberg excerpts taken from <u>Epicenter</u> (Carol Stream, Illinois: Tyndale House Publishers, Inc., Copyright 2006) page x. Used by permission of Tyndale House Publishers, Inc., All rights Reserved.

7. Ibid., page xiii.

8. Slobodan Lekic, Associated Press Writer, "Iran's Ahmadinejad: US 'Empire' Nears Collapse" Associated Press Release, September 23, 2008, (http://abcnews.go.com/US/wireStory?id=5863414), Used with permission of The Associated Press Copyright 2009. All rights reserved.

9. Ezekiel 38.

10. Ezekiel 39: 12.

11. Ezekiel 39: 9.

12. Daniel 9: 27.

13. Stephen R. Miller, excerpts taken from <u>The New American Commentary</u>, Daniel Volume 18, page 271. Used by Permission.

14. Matthew 24:15; Daniel 9:27; 2 Thessalonians 2: 4.

15. Stephen R. Miller, excerpts taken from <u>The New American Commentary</u>, Daniel Volume 18, page 273. Used by Permission.

16. Randall Price, excerpts taken from <u>The Temple and Bible Prophecy,</u> (Eugene Oregon 97402: Harvest House Publishers, Copyright 1999/2005 by World of the Bible ministries, Inc. <u>www.harvesthousepublishers.com</u>,) page 496. Used by Permission of Harvest House publishers.

17. Thomas Ice and Timothy Demy, excerpts taken from <u>The Truth about the Last Days Temple</u> (Eugene Oregon 97402: Harvest House Publishers, Copyright 1997) page 29. Used with permission of Harvest House Publishers.

18. Ibid., page 30.

19. Daniel 12:4.

20. Matthew 24:32-34.

Chapter 10 The Clock Is Ticking -Again

1. Revelation 13:11-12.

2. Revelation 17: 13, 17.

3. Revelation 4:1.

4. Revelation 5:1.

5. Revelation 6:2.

6. Revelation 6:4, 14.

7. Revelation 6: 5, 6.

8. Matthew 20: 2-9.

9. Revelation 6: 8.

10. Isaiah 24:19, 20.

11. Revelation 6:12-14.

12. Revelation 6: 13-17.

13. Richard Stone, "Target Earth" <u>National Geographic.Com /Magazine,</u> August 2008, Volume 214- No 2, Page142, Used by permission.

14. Ibid., page 138.

Chapter 11 The Good, The Bad, and The Ugly

1. Revelation 8:1.

2. Revelation 8:7.

3. Revelation 8: 8.

4. Revelation 8:10.

5. Revelation 8:12.

Chapter 12 The "Dark Side"

1. Revelation 9:1.

2. Revelation 9:2, 3.

3. 2 Peter 2:4.

4. Revelation 9:14-21.

Chapter 13 Last Call

1. Revelation 7: 4.

2. Revelation 11:3-11.

3. Revelation 7: 9-12.

4. Vaughn Aubuchon, "World Population Growth History" Page 1/3, http://www.pagers.vaughns-1-pagers.com/history/world-com/history/world-population-growth.htm, Used by permission of Vaughn Aubuchon.

5. Revelation 14:6-11; Revelation 10:6-7.

Chapter 14 It's Gonna Get Ugly

1. Isaiah 14:12-14.

2. Revelation 12: 10.

3. Revelation 13:3, 14.

4. John Phillips, excerpts taken from Exploring Revelation, (Grand Rapids, Michigan: Published by Kregel Publications, Copyright 1987) page 166Used by permission of the publisher. All rights reserved.

5. Revelation17:8.

6. Revelation 13:3.

7. John F Walvoord with Mark Hitchcock, excerpts from
    Armageddon, Oil and Terror, Used by permission of Tyndale
    House Publishers, Inc. All rights reserved, page 129.

8. Randall Price, excerpts taken from The Temple and
    Bible Prophecy, Used with Permission of harvest House
    publishers, page 496.

9. Zechariah 13:8-9.

10. Daniel 12:11.

11. Revelation 12:14.

12. Exodus 19:4.

13. Tim La Haye, excerpts from Revelation Illustrated and
    Made Plain. Used by permission of Zondervan Publishing
    House, page 164.

14. Isaiah 63:1.

15. Photograph of the tombs in Petra, Edom located in modern
    Jordan, by Steve Maricelli, Used by permission.

16. Photograph of the Treasury in Petra, Edom located
    in modern Jordan, by Sammie Maricelli, Used by
    permission.

Chapter 15 The Pin

1. Revelation 11:10.

2. Revelation 11: 7-12.

3. Revelation 13: 16-18.

4. Associated Press Release, November 11, 2008,
    "Congressman: Obama Wants Gestapo-like Force"
    (http://www.msnbc.msn.com/id/27655039/). Used with
    permission of The Associated Press Copyright 2008. All
    rights reserved.

5. Revelation13:14.

6. Revelation Chapter 13: 15.

7. Revelation Chapter 13:15.

8. Revelation Chapter 20: 4.

9. Source model builder and photographer, Michael (http://en.wikipedia.org/wiki/File:Guillotinemodels.jpg), Used by permission of Michael.

Chapter 16 Tale of Two Cities

1. Revelation 16:2.

2. Revelation 16:3.

3. Revelation 16:4.

4. Revelation 16:8.

5. Revelation 16:10.

6. Revelation 17:1.

7. Hal Lindsey, excerpts from Apocalypse Code, (Palos Verdes California: Western front Ltd., Copyright 1997) page 200, Used with permission of Hal Lindsey.

8. Ezekiel 16: 1-17.

9. Tim La Haye, excerpts from Revelation Illustrated and Made Plain, Used by permission of Zondervan Publishing House, page 234.

10. Revelation17: 11.

11. John Phillips, excerpts taken from Exploring Revelation, Used by permission of the publisher. All rights reserved, page 215.

12. Ibid., Page 206.

13. Clarence Larkin, excerpts taken from Dispensational Truth. (Philadelphia: Rev. Clarence Larkin Estate, Copyright 1920) page 140. Used by permission of The Rev. Clarence Larkin Estate, P.O. Box 33, Glenside, Pa.19038, U.S.A.215-576-5590 (http://www.larkinestate.com).

14. John Phillips, excerpts taken from <u>Exploring Revelation,</u> Used by permission of the publisher. All rights reserved. Page 206.

15. Tim La Haye excerpts taken from <u>Revelation Illustrated and Made Plain</u>, page 234. Used by permission of Zondervan Publishing House.

16. Revelation 17:16, 17.

17. John Phillips excerpts taken from <u>Exploring Revelation,</u> Used by permission of the publisher. All rights reserved, page 218.

18. Tim La Haye, excerpts taken from <u>Revelation Illustrated and Made Plain</u> page 236. Used by permission of Zondervan Publishing House.

19. Daniel 7:8.

Chapter 17 Death Valley

1. Revelation16: 13-14.

2. Revelation 16:14, 16.

3. Adrian Rogers, excerpts taken from <u>Unveiling the End Times in Our Time</u>, (Nashville, Tennessee: Broadman and Holman Publishers, Copyright 2004) page 222-223. Used by permission. All rights reserved.

4. Isaiah 63:1-3.

5. Joel 3:2.

6. Zechariah 12:9

7. Revelation 16:12.

8. Revelation 18: 2, 10, 18, 19.

9. Hal Lindsey, excerpts taken from <u>Apocalypse Code,</u> page 215, 216, Used with permission of Hal Lindsey.

10. Revelation 18:10, 15, 17, 18.

11. Revelation 18: 8, 19.

Chapter 18 Armageddon

1. Revelation 19:12.

2. Revelation 19:17-18.

3. Tim La Haye and Jerry B. Jenkins, excerpts taken from <u>Are We Living in the End Times</u>? (Carol Stream: Illinois, Copyright 1999 by Tim La Haye and Jerry B. Jenkins). Page 228. Used by permission of Tyndal House Publishers, Inc. All rights reserved.

4. Amos8: 9.

5. Joel 2: 31.

6. Matthew 24: 29-30.

7. Revelation 19: 15, 21.

8. Zechariah 14: 12.

9. Revelation 14:20.

10. Revelation 16: 19.

11. Revelation 16: 21.

12. Acts 1: 11-12.

13. Zechariah 14: 4.

14. Revelation 16: 18.

15. Zechariah 14: 13, 15.

16. Zechariah 14: 7.

17. Revelation 19: 20.

Chapter 19 The Key to The Secret

1. Luke 2:4-12.

2. Romans 3:23.

3. Romans 6: 23.

4. John 3: 16.

5. Ephesians 2: 8.

6. Romans 10: 9.

7.   Romans 8: 35-39.

8.   Matthew 18:10.

9.   Matthew 16: 18.

10. Acts 2:42.

11. Dianne Frances Donenfeld "Twas the Night Before Jesus Came," *Serving God Is My Business.*

Chapter 20 Tick, Tock…

1.   Evelyn Husband with Donna Van Liere, excerpts taken from <u>High Calling</u> page 197, "Reprinted by permission, all rights reserved."

2.   Revelation 21: 27; Revelation 20:12.

3.   John 14: 3.

4.   Revelation 22: 5.

5.   Matthew 22: 28-30.

6.   Luke 9: 28-33.

7.   Revelation 7:17; Revelation 21: 4.

8.   Isaiah 65: 17-19.

CPSIA information can be obtained at www.ICGtesting.com
Printed in the USA
LVOW092333061211

258127LV00001B/2/P